Real Country Humor

T0168244

REAL COUNTRY HUMOR

Jokes From
Country Music
Personalities

Collected and edited by
Billy Edd Wheeler

August House Publishers, Inc.
LITTLE ROCK

Published 2002 by August House Publishers, Inc.
P.O. Box 3223, Little Rock, Arkansas, 72203,
501-372-5450
http://www.augusthouse.com

Printed in the United States of America

10   9   8   7   6   5   4   3   2   1

The paper used in this publication meets the minimum requirements of
the American National Standard for Information Sciences—Permanence of
Paper for Printed Library Materials, ANSI Z39.48-1984.

*On the cover (left to right): Steve Wariner, Patsy Cline,
Chet Atkins (photo by David Michael Kennedy, used by permission
of Sony Music Nashville), Vince Gill and Dolly Parton
(photo by Chris Hollo), Jerry Reed*

AUGUST HOUSE   PUBLISHERS   LITTLE ROCK

for Chet Atkins, C.G.P.
JUNE 20, 1924-JUNE 30, 2001

Thanks, Chet, for thirty-five fun years of shared humor—jokes, anecdotes, and hilarious true tales. In spite of calling yourself a "semi-celebrity," you were the greatest celebrity and celebrity-maker of them all—the world's best all-around guitarist and the funniest and classiest guy I ever knew. As our friend Bob Jennings used to say, "I'm glad God put me on this earth at the same time Chet Atkins was here." (Amen, Bob.)

ACKNOWLEDGMENTS

Thanks to:

Ted and Liz Parkhurst, for spotting this book embedded in a rejected book proposal, for their challenge to make it happen, and for Liz's contributions to concept, format, and hands-on support and feedback during the writing process.

Teresa K. Tatham, for research and bios, joke summaries, and for proofreading several versions of the manuscript.

All my contributors, for jokes, anecdotes, funny stories, reminiscences, and photographs. You made it a fun project.

Tandy Rice, for getting me in touch with his clients, George Lindsey, T. Bubba Bechtol, and the estate of Jerry Clower.

Scott Siman, for the joke from his young client, Billy Gilman.

Mark Ford, for his help at NSAI with addresses; Robert Harris, communications assistant at *CMA Close Up*; and Chris Hollo, for the photo of Vince Gill and Dolly Parton.

Merle Kilgore, for material on Hank Williams Sr.; Don Robertson, for material on Elvis; Charlie Dick, for material on Patsy Cline; and "ProJoe" Taggert, for connecting me with his golfing buddy, Vince Gill.

Linda Dotson, for jokes, photos, and material from Sheb Wooley.

Paul Craft, for jokes, songs, and help in securing permission to use copyrighted materials.

My wife Mary, daughter Lucy, and son Travis, for letting me try the jokes out on them.

CONTENTS

INTRODUCTION

"It all begins with a song."

That slogan, if you're a songwriter, is more than just a pretty catchphrase. It has the ring of truth. I've been hearing it since I moved to Nashville in 1968 to manage the offices of United Artists Music Group. In 1971, I was invited to speak at the awards banquet of the organization that adopted the slogan as its own, NSAI, the Nashville Songwriters Association International.

The year before, Kris Kristofferson had been named NSAI's Songwriter of the Year for "For the Good Times," the #1 smash for Ray Price. Kris went on to write "Me and Bobby McGee," recorded by Janis Joplin; "Help Me Make It Through The Night," a hit for Sammi Smith; "Sunday Morning Coming Down," recorded by Johnny Cash; and many other great songs. Six years later, he would be inducted into NSAI's Hall of Fame.

At the time, I had only had a song that went to #2 in *Billboard,* "Ode To The Little Brown Shack Out Back," and a top ten record by The Kingston Trio in 1963, "The Rev. Mr. Black." Hardly enough to make me a candidate for NSAI's Hall of Fame, or even Songwriter of the Year.

It would take me twenty-five years just to get nominated. And after being nominated two more times and failing to get inducted, I didn't experience a racing pulse when I was nominated for the fourth time in 2000. In fact, I hadn't even planned to attend the awards banquet, strongly suspecting I would fail yet again.

I told my wife Mary, daughter Lucy, and son Travis I wasn't going to make it. I said, "They always give you a hint if you're going in, to make sure you'll be there, and I haven't had any hints. Besides, I'm up against Allen Reynolds. He's not only written some fabulous songs, he produces Garth Brooks, Kathy Mattea, Crystal Gayle, and Don Williams. He's strong as a bear's breath."

I was about to send my regrets when I received an e-mail from Liz Parkhurst, the co-big wheel at August House Publishers. She and her husband Ted had spotted a book embedded in a proposal of mine they'd rejected—a chapter entitled "Real Country Humor: Jokes From Country Music Personalities."

Liz said, "Are you interested?"

Was I interested? Does an accordion player wear rings and play "Lady of Spain"?

A flash of inspiration hit me. I would go to NSAI's Hall of Fame banquet and use the occasion to gather jokes. After all, some pretty big names were nominated this year in addition to Allen Reynolds, not to mention dozens of songwriters who'd be there wearing red roses signifying they'd already made it into the Hall. "You'll have a big pool to fish in," Liz reminded me when I told her about my nomination.

The Common Ingredient among Country Music Makers

This got me to thinking about what I'd say in this introduction, and it didn't take me long to decide on a theme. As in every profession, the music business has tons of talented people behind the scenes, behind the icons. But what setting would bring the most of them together, the place where "the creative rubber hits the road," so to speak, where the nitty-gritty of making music is at its most intense, most enjoyable, most quixotic?

The studio.

Seems to me, country-music makers have one thing in common, in addition to their love of good songs, good picking and singing, and appreciative fans. They love jokes and funny stories. This gets me to the studio.

It is impossible to attend a recording session in Nashville without hearing lots of jokes. Nashville cats love to laugh. And every group of music makers coming into the studio seems to have its own brand of humor. The way recordings are made today, typically speaking, it's done in several stages:

One: You begin with the rhythm section—piano, bass, guitar, and drums. These guys laugh and joke a lot to break the tension between takes as they lay down the original tracks. While the arranger or session leader is listening to a playback, or during a break between songs, one of these pickers will share a goodie, perhaps introducing it as "a joke like nun other":

> Two nuns are asked to paint a room in the convent, and the last instruction of the Mother Superior is that they not get even a drop of paint on their habits. After conferring for a bit the nuns decide to lock the door, strip off their habits, and paint in the nude. In the middle of the project there comes a knock at the door. "Who is it?" calls one of the nuns. "Blind man," replies a voice from the other side of the door. The nuns shrug and decide that no harm can come from letting a blind man into the room, so they open the door. "Nice boobs," says the man. "Where do you want these blinds?"

Two: Then the "color" musicians come in and overdub lead guitars, fiddle and mandolin breaks, keyboard pads, and sweetenings.

These too are gifted studio musicians and usually work fast, their fingers keeping just ahead of their humorous quips and one-liners. They often poke fun at each other with question-and-answer routines:

> **Q:** How many drummers does it take to screw in a light bulb?
> **A:** None. They have machines that can do that now.

> **Q:** What do you throw a drowning guitar player?
> **A:** His amp.

> **Q:** What's the saddest thing about five entertainment lawyers driving a Buick over a cliff?
> **A:** A Buick holds six.

> **Q:** What was the last thing the drummer said before he got kicked out of the band?
> **A:** "Hey, I wrote some lyrics last night."

> **Q:** How do you stop the spread of AIDS?
> **A:** Let BMG distribute it.

During the last session I produced, this whirlwind named Jonathan Yudkin breezes into the studio firing on all cylinders, cracking joke after joke between his dazzling mandolin and fiddle work. After doubling us over with Jewish mother jokes and other assorted vignettes, he tells us one about a one-man welcoming committee:

> This guy hadn't been in town long until a neighbor drops in and invites him to a party, a getting-to-know-you affair. He said, "Come on over Saturday. We'll cook a little, drink a little, maybe sing and dance, have some sex, whoop and holler—just have a big old time." The new guy said it sounded like fun and asked what he

should wear. The neighbor says, "Doesn't matter. It's just you and me!"

Three: If there are strings on the session, the string players—many of whom are probably moonlighting members of the Nashville Symphony—use humor that can be a little subtler. For instance, the *Washington Post*'s "Style Invitational" asks readers to take any word from the dictionary, alter it by adding, subtracting, or changing one letter, and supply a new definition. I could see these being some of the string players' favorites:

Foreploy: Any misrepresentation about yourself for the purpose of obtaining sex.

Tatyr: A lecherous Mr. Potato Head.

Giraffiti: Vandalism spray-painted very, very high, such as on an overpass.

Sarchasm: The gulf between the author of sarcastic wit and the recipient who doesn't get it.

Contratemps: The resentment permanent workers feel toward the fill-in workers.

Reintarnation: Coming back to life as a hillbilly.

Hipatitis: Terminal coolness.

Guillozine: A magazine for executioners.

Karmageddon: It's like, when everybody is sending off all these really bad vibes, right? And then, like, the earth explodes and it's like a really serious bummer.

Glibido: All talk and no action.

When the string players tire of the word games they might invade the color musicians' territory:

> **Q:** How many booking agents does it take to screw in a light bulb?
> **A:** Listen, I'll call you back next week if I have an answer.

> **Q:** How do you get a guitar player to turn down?
> **A:** Put sheet music in front of him.

(Back when Chet Atkins was playing guitar on sessions—before he became head of RCA Records in Nashville—a New York producer once asked him, "Do you read music?" Chet's reply: "Yeah, but I try not to let it get in the way of my picking.")

> **Q:** What do you call a guitar player who only knows two chords?
> **A:** A music critic.

> **Q:** What is the last thing a topless dancer does with her asshole before she goes to work?
> **A:** Drops him off at rehearsal.

> **Q:** What's the difference between a good ol' boy and a redneck?
> **A:** The good ol' boy raises livestock. The redneck gets emotionally involved.

> **Q:** What does a drummer say when he knocks at your door?
> **A:** "Pizza."

St. Peter's IQ Test

Three men are killed in a tragic auto accident. As they approach St. Peter, he asks each one the same question. "How high is your IQ?" The first replies, "130." St. Peter says to him, "Fine, fine. Go back to earth and be a chemical engineer." The second replies, "125." St Peter says, "Fine, fine. Go back to earth and be a lawyer." The third replies, "I dunno . . . 'bout 80, I reckon." St. Peter says to him, "Fine, fine—uh, what brand of sticks do you use?"

Four: Next comes the star or the featured artist to lay down the lead vocals. He or she will relay some new jokes they heard on the West Coast or in England, down in Texas or up in Maine. Everybody laughs when the stars tell jokes, but only if they're funny. Remember, this is Nashville. Studio musicians are not overly impressed with stars. (A lot of stars started out as studio musicians or background vocalists.)

One of the superstars who had a big hit with a song I co-wrote with Roger Bowling, "Coward of the County," was Kenny Rogers, the master storyteller. In the movie version, Kenny played the uncle who told his nephew's story, the kid the whole county thought was a coward. The boy's dad, who died in prison, begged him to walk away from trouble, saying, "It won't mean you're weak if you turn the other cheek / I hope you're old enough to understand—son, you don't have to fight to be a man."

Kenny played a preacher who not only liked whiskey and fraternized with women, he also had a keen sense of humor. One Sunday while in the pulpit preaching, he told a joke to illustrate a point:

Somebody stole the preacher's bike, or at least he thought so. On the other hand, he had a bad memory, so it crossed his mind he might have left it somewhere. He decided to preach a sermon on the Ten Commandments and concentrate hard on "Thou shalt not steal," keeping his eye on potential thieves sitting in the congregation. If one of them shifted around nervously in the pew, or broke out in a sweat, he'd have a likely suspect. He bore down hard. "It's a sin to steal!" But nobody flinched. So he moved on, and when he got to "Thou shalt not commit adultery," he remembered where he'd left his bike."

Several country music stars are known for their wonderful sense of humor: Dolly Parton, Ray Stevens, Ralph Emery, June Carter Cash, Mel Tillis, Mike Snider, Sheb Wooley, Jeff Foxworthy, Roni Stoneman, Jimmy Dean—the late and greats: Minnie Pearl, Archie Campbell, Grandpa Jones, Jerry Clower, Merle Travis—and many more, living and dead. Jerry Reed told me he couldn't do a show without telling jokes. He has to get next to the audience. Laughing and having fun is who he is, as much as songwriting, singing, and his fantastic guitar playing.

Five: Finally, the background vocalists put the finishing touches on the tracks, oohhing and aahhing or singing along with the artist. They work hard, these extraordinary talents, and they're quick studies. They have to be, working under the gun while the producer watches the clock—they don't come cheap—and they're worth every penny. They add the icing to the cake, wrapping their warm tones around the star's vocal until he or she sounds like the Magi surrounded by angels.

Usually working as a twosome, sometimes as a foursome, two

women and two men, their voices are often "stacked" until they end up sounding like the Mormon Tabernacle Choir. During breaks the guys talk golf while the women talk kids or dates or husbands. Dana McVickers told this one:

> This woman asked her husband when he was going to fix the broken telephone. He said, "Do I look like Alexander Graham Bell?" That night she asked him when he was going to fix the reading lamp on her side of the bed. His curt reply was, "Do I look like Thomas Edison?" The following week when he came home from work one afternoon, his wife said, "Honey, don't worry about fixing the telephone or the reading lamp. Our neighbor John came over today and took care of it, fixed them both." Her husband asked how much John charged for doing all that work. She said, "He was so nice—he said I could either bake him a cake or he'd take it out in trade." The husband said, "What kind of cake did you bake him?" She smiled and replied, "Do I look like Betty Crocker?"

Does that story sound like song material? It is. It was. Paul Craft and I wrote it several years ago. We called it, "What I Look Like To You," and it is featured in the "Funny Country Songs" section.

Roger Miller once remarked that songwriters are like butterfly catchers—their nets are always at the ready in case an idea flutters by. Joke butterflies come ready made for songs. Paul Craft netted another good one in his "It's Me Again, Margaret," a hit for Ray Stevens. (The joke was told by Nashville publisher/producer Ray Baker; the song is included here in the "Funny Country Songs" section.) Lee Roy Parnell and Tony Haselden snagged a dandy that turned into a hit for Collin Ray:

George comes home at 4:00 A.M. and tries to sneak past his wife with his shoes in his hand. She's a light sleeper, though, and raises up to demand where he's been all night. Anticipating this, he says, "Well honey, I came home about 11:30 and didn't want to come up here and wake you up, so I went to sleep in the hammock down on the porch." "George," she said sternly, "I put the hammock in the attic three weeks ago." "Well," he replied, a bit flustered, "That's my story and I'm sticking to it!"

Of course, part of that punch line—"That's My Story"—became the title of the song, which further popularized the phrase until it has been adopted into everyday speech. Chet Atkins and I wrote a song based on a joke that appears later in the book, an old tale collected in the Ozarks by noted folklorist Vance Randolph. He called his "Pissing In The Snow." We call ours "I Still Write Your Name In The Snow."

Back to NSAI's Hall of Fame Banquet

When I arrived at the Loew's Vanderbilt Plaza Hotel, I had my Olympus microcassette recorder handy. Among the six hundred songwriters, artists, publishers and other music biz executives I spotted several nominees wearing white roses like mine—Mac Davis, who wrote "In The Ghetto" and "Baby, Don't Get Hooked On Me"; Randy Goodrum, who wrote "You Needed Me" and "Bluer Than Blue"; and Larry Henley, who wrote "The Wind Beneath My Wings." Quicker on the draw than Billy the Kid, I reached into the inside pocket of my tux and managed to corner all of them for a joke.

Among the august group wearing red roses I caught up with Bobby Braddock—two-time CMA Song Of The Year award winner for "He Stopped Loving Her Today"; Glenn Sutton, who wrote "Almost Persuaded" and "My Elusive Dreams"; and Jack "Cowboy" Clement, a Nashville genius who discovered Charley Pride and other artists, and wrote "Miller's Cave" and "Just Someone I Used To Know." They all gave me jokes that appear in the pages that follow.

I thought, *Wow, Liz Parkhurst was right, this is a great pond to fish in, and I've hooked some keepers. Who cares about that old hand-holding-the-quill trophy they give you when you're inducted?* That was my mindset. Imagine the surprise (the shock) when Jerry Chesnut was called to the podium to welcome me into the Hall of Fame, as the band played my songs "Jackson" and "Coward of the County." Then the double surprise of finding Lucy and Mary waiting with celebratory hugs when I returned to my table. They'd snuck into town and got a room at the Loew's Vanderbilt Plaza, at three hundred dollars, while I bunked in the boonies at forty-one.

Allen Reynolds and I tied, by the way, so they saved him until last. The audience was delighted—so was my daughter—when a surprise guest artist named Garth Brooks suddenly appeared to sing a medley of Allen's songs: "I Recall A Gypsy Woman," "Wrong Road Again," and "Somebody Loves You." Lucy got her picture taken with him, and although I didn't get a joke from him, it was a night to remember.

So here I sit typing the jokes I captured on tape, hoping you'll have as much fun reading them as I did collecting them while champagne flowed and cameras flashed that evening. The other jokes were given to me directly or on the phone, sent by tape, snail mail, and e-mail. Some of the contributors are not well known by the general public, but their songs and productions are. In the country-music community they are celebrated personalities, characters, and legends. After all, where would stars be without songs to sing? And where would songwriters be without singers to sing their songs? It's a symbiotic relationship.

From my point of view, NSAI's long-time slogan, "It all begins with a song," might just as well be, "It all begins with a joke." Humor was the catalyst that brought Chet Atkins and me together. He used to invite people to his office at RCA Records at the end of the day—Norro Wilson, Howard White, Jerry Reed, Bob Jennings, and many others—to yuk it up before going home to supper. Luckily, I was next door at United Artists Music Group, and when he whistled I came running. Memories of those laugh sessions are among my richest treasures.

So here, all you joke lovers, have a laugh on us.

—*Billy Edd Wheeler*

Please note: If a rose appears beside the name of the following contributors, it means they have been inducted into NSAI's Hall of Fame.

Drinking and Carousing

Ray Stevens

" I'll ride up here on the roof. If we get stopped, tell 'em I'm a pair of skis." **"**

*—the late Townes Van Zandt
to Danna Garcia, in Canyon, Texas,
heading for an after-the-gig
party in a packed car*

The Day That Leroy Drowned

by Sheb Wooley 🌹
(recorded by Ray Stevens as
"The Day That Clancy Drowned")

In the town of Old Milwaukee, back in 1982,
He celebrated forty years of making that famous brew.
Leroy, the champion taster, Milwaukee's number one,
He could feel the flavor when it swished across his tongue.
Overtime and weekends, old Leroy never shirked;
They said it was amazing how much he loved his work.
But one scorching afternoon as he made his final round,
He slipped into a vat of beer and poor old Leroy drowned.

CHORUS #1
Oh the day that Leroy drowned . . .
He could have called for help, but Lord, he never made a sound.
We tried to rescue him but we didn't have no luck,
'Cause he'd dive to the bottom and we couldn't pull him up.

It was a solemn occasion as his buddies gathered 'round;
We had to make arrangements for to put him in the ground.
When we took the dear departed over to the funeral place;
It took 'em half an hour to get that big smile off his face.
Brother Daniels preached the funeral and had some words to say
About the life of Brother Leroy, and how he passed away.
Could it not have been avoided that he met his tragic end?
Well, preacher, he got up three times and went to the bathroom,
But he always jumped back in.

CHORUS #2

Oh, the day that Leroy drowned . . .

He was blowing pretty bubbles and swimming all around;

A-gurgling and a-giggling and a-wearing that silly grin,

But he fought us like a flounder when we tried to pull him in.

A Tale of Two Tipplers

They were obviously smashed, and after eyeing each other for a few moments one said to the other, "Pardon me, but you look Irish. Are ye from Ireland, by any chance?"

"Why, yes, I am. I'm from Dublin," the man said.

"Ain't that something, now, so am I. I graduated from Public School Number 65 in 1963."

"How about that!" the man replied again. "So did I. Same school, same year."

As the conversation continued and the coincidences mounted, they grew more excited, laughing and toasting and slapping each other on the back.

Another man walked into the bar, ordered a drink and said, "What's happening?"

The bartender said, "The O'Malley twins are commode-hugging drunk again."

—*Ray Stevens* 🌹

The Reluctant Samaritan

A drunk's car breaks down, so he knocks on this man's door and asks for a push. The man tells him to get lost, slams the door, and goes back to bed. He tells his wife about it, and she says, "You ought to be more charitable. You might be in that same situation yourself sometime." So he goes back down, opens the door, and doesn't see the guy. Then he hears a voice calling out, "I'm over here—in the swing."

—Jack "Cowboy" Clement 🌹

(It took me a minute to catch that one, too. —Ed.)

Musical Beds

Two drunks checked into a hotel and were given a room with two double beds. They got undressed, turned off the light, and both got into the same bed. One of them said, "Are you all right?"

The other one said, "No, there's somebody in bed with me."

The first one rolled over and said, "There's somebody in bed with me too."

"Let's count to three and throw them out," the other one said. So they counted to three, there was a great commotion, and one of them hit the floor.

The one in bed said, "Are you all right?"

His buddy said, "No, he threw me out."

"That's all right," the one in bed said. "Come on, you can get up here with me."

—Archie Campbell

A Taste Of Shine

I was raised out in Frick, Oklahoma, and one night this guy came home with a jar of moonshine. His wife ambushed him. "I want to see what's in this stuff that makes you like it so much." She grabbed the jar and chug-a-lugged a big old swallow, lost her breath, coughed, turned red, did a double back flip and sputtered, "Lord a-mercy, this stuff tastes terrible!" Her old man gazed her into focus and said, "See there. And all this time, I'll bet you thought I was enjoying it!"

—*Roger Miller* 🌹

Uppity People

An ex-coal miner from Muhlenberg County, Kentucky, went up to Cincinnati to find some work. He was a fun-loving, good-hearted sort of fellow, but he wouldn't take anything off of anybody. When he got there he went into a bar where they had a five-hundred-pound gorilla for a bouncer.

The Kentuckian drank a few drinks and got to singing some of the old murder ballads from the hills. The owner got tired of it after a while and asked him to shut up, but he kept on singing and carrying on. So the owner unchained the gorilla, which went over and grabbed the miner and carried him outside.

There was a lot of commotion out there, with noises of scuffling and grunting and banging around. Finally, the coal miner came back in. "Lordy," he said, "give some people a fur coat and they think they own the place!"

—*Merle Travis*

What the Drunk Man Saw

A drunk man staggers into the ladies' restroom at a bar, quite by mistake. And all would be fine, except there's a drunk old barfly in there, worshipping the porcelain gods. Her ample bosom has shaken loose from her skimpy bra, so that her boobs are dangling just above the water in the bowl with every heave she heaves.

Looking on, the drunk man finally has to say something. "Lady," he slurs, "if you're gonna drown them puppies anyway, I'd sure like to have that big one with the pink nose!"

—Juni Fisher

Alien Thieves

A police car cruising by a late-night bar sees a fellow with his pants down around his ankles, waving a car key drunkenly at the empty air.

One of the officers gets out and approaches him saying, "Sir, what are you doing with that car key?"

The drunk blearily replies, "Aliens stole my car! Aliens stole my car!"

This gives the policeman a moment's pause. He studies the man trying to start an invisible car and says, "Sir, do you realize your pants are down and your privates are hanging out for all the world to see?"

The drunk gasps, looks down at his excitement, stares wildly at the cop and says, "Oh Lord, they got Julie too!"

—Janis Ian

Faron Young and Dick's Drive-In

About ten years before Faron Young died, we were playing in the Acuff-Rose Golf Tournament down at Henry Horton State Park. Because we registered late, there was no room left at the park's inn. Faron and I ended up at a motel in Lewisburg, fifteen miles away. After having a few drinks and swapping a lot of jokes—or a lot of drinks and a few jokes— we decided we were hungry.

We found a place called Dick's Drive-In. It was closed, but the lights were still on, so I banged on the door until a rough-looking man in a greasy apron appeared. "What's going on?" he asked.

"I've got Faron Young with me, there in his Cadillac, and he's hungry as I am," I said.

He stared out at the car, obviously skeptical. "That ain't Faron Young!" he said in a loud voice. Faron heard him and was out of the car in a flash. "You cock-lip son of a blankety-blank *?!#%:<&~%, who in the hell do you think I am?" He strutted up like a banty rooster.

The man blinked, then smiled. "That is Faron, ain't it?" He pushed the door open wide and said, "You'uns come on in. I'm Dick." He held out a big greasy paw. Faron and I shook his hand and stepped inside. They took a few chairs off the tables, Dick fired up his grill, and while Faron and I sang songs to the giggling wait staff, Dick cooked us the best fish sand-wiches I had ever eaten. "I got some bourbon hid back yon-der in the freezer," Dick said, "in between some hamburger patties. All I got to mix it with is Sprite, but, do you'uns want a drink?" His eyes twinkled. We said we did.

We told people about it at the golf tournament the next day, and that night the place was packed. Faron and I were pleased. Going to Dick's Drive-In became a tradition.

—Billy Edd Wheeler 🌹

Not the Sharpest Knife in the Drawer

Billy Edd Wheeler

When the Lord handed out brains, I thought He said trains and caught the wrong one!

—*Billy Edd Wheeler* 🌹

Babies, Not Bugs

In the backwoods of Tennessee, the redneck's wife went into labor in the middle of the night. The doctor was called out to assist in the delivery. Since there was no electricity, the doctor handed the father-to-be a lantern and said, "Here, you hold this high so I can see what I'm doing."

Soon a baby boy was brought into the world and the redneck was putting down the light and reaching for the baby. "Whoa, there," the doctor said. "Don't be in a rush to put the lantern down. I think there's yet another one to come."

Sure enough, within minutes he had delivered a baby girl.

"No, no, don't be in a great hurry to be setting down that lantern," cried the doctor. "It seems there's another one on the way."

The redneck scratched his head in bewilderment and asked the doctor, "Do you reckon it's the light that's attractin' 'em?"

—*Dolly Parton* 🌹

A Sense of Place

A blonde goes into the library and says, "I'd like a cheeseburger, fries, and a coke." The librarian informs her that she's in a library. So the blonde says, whispering, "I'd like a cheeseburger, fries, and a coke."

—*Jack "Cowboy" Clement* 🌹

Slow on the Draw

There was this woman who talked so slow that before she could say she wasn't that kind of woman, she was.

—*Minnie Pearl*

Tales from Jasper, Alabama

I know a guy in my hometown of Jasper, Alabama, that thinks the Betty Ford Center is a place to get your car fixed.

I told him with that kind of intelligence he should have a Ph.D. He said, "I already got a post hole digger."

He's the one that listens to the radio every Fourth of July to hear the fireworks.

When I asked him what he'd been doing, he said, "Well, I was just in my first earthquake, and it so happened, when it hit, my wife and me was in bed making love." I asked him if he got hurt. "Naw," he said, "it just threw me on the floor and almost woke her up!"

The first time he saw an escalator, he run up to the store clerk and said, "If you don't stop that thing you're going to have a basement full of steps!"

—*George Lindsey*

The Irishman's Two Wishes

An Irishman was sitting by the seaside daydreaming one day, when a genie appeared and said to him, "Today's your lucky day, my man. I've come to offer you two wishes."

"Two wishes? Really?"

The genie nodded, and asked him what his first wish was. The Irishman thought for a moment, then said, "I'd like a pint glass full of Guinness, and no matter how much I drank, it would keep refilling itself."

The genie said, "No problem," snapped his fingers and *poof!* There was a pint glass that filled up with Guinness. The man drank it down, and immediately it filled back up again. He was amazed.

The genie asked, "Do you have another wish?"

The Irishman thought a minute, and said, "Yeah, I'll have another one of those!"

—*Randy Goodrum*

Birth Control with a Bang

A couple decided, after eleven kids, they didn't want to have any more, so the husband went to the doctor and told him that he and his cousin were through with makin' young'uns. He wanted to get things fixed up so's they wouldn't have any more.

The doctor described the traditional vasectomy procedure, stated a price, and the man thought for a minute. "Ain't you got anything what don't cost so much, and don't involve a knife?" he asked.

"Well," the doctor replied, "we do have another easier, faster way, and it won't cost nearly as much. Go get you a can of Pabst Blue Ribbon and drink it down fast. Then get you a cherry bomb, light it, and drop it in the hole in the can. Hold the can and count to ten. Works like a charm."

"Hey now, Doc," the man said, "I don't want to ask no stupid questions, but how can that work?"

"Just trust me," the doctor replied. "It'll work."

The fellow goes down to the store, buys a can of Pabst Blue Ribbon, and chugs it down, like he's supposed to. Then he goes back in and buys a cherry bomb. He takes it back to the truck, so's he has a place to sit down to work on the project, lights the cherry bomb, drops it in the can, holds the can in one hand and counts to five. Then he sets the can between his legs, so he can go on counting . . .

—*Juni Fisher*

A Patriot Faces Death

A man goes to the doctor and says, "Doctor, I haven't been feeling well in a while."

The doctor examines him and says, "No wonder you're not feeling well. You have only two weeks to live."

The man says, "Oh, my God, only two weeks to live? Wow, I've got so much to do and so little time to do it. Well, then, first I've got to join the Communist party, and then . . . "

The doctor interrupts. "You mean to tell me that with only two weeks to live, you, an American citizen, are going to join the Communist party? Why?"

"I'm very patriotic, Doc," the man says. "It's better one of them should die than one of us!"

—Larry Henley

Religion

Jerry Reed

66 One good thing you can say about the Devil: He's always on the job. 99

—*Billy Edd Wheeler* 🌺

The Biggest Draw of All

More than twenty-five thousand came to see "flights of angels sing Hank Williams to his rest," to misquote Shakespeare. The funeral was on January 4, 1953, in Montgomery, Alabama. Horace Logan, Program Director of KWKH, and head of the *Louisiana Hayride,* flew down for the services with Felton Pruett, one of Hank's early steel guitarists, *Louisiana Hayride* guitarist Dobber Johnson, and a few others. Opry Manager Jim Denny, who had fired Hank from the Opry, sat near Logan. He said, "Logan, if Hank could raise up in his coffin, he'd look up toward this stage and say, 'I told you dumb sons-of-bitches I could draw more dead than you could alive!'"

—*Merle Kilgore*

The Preacher and Little Billy

This country preacher down in Texas was all wound up in his sermon, and he was saying, "Oh, brothers and sisters, it's gonna be a good week, I know it is. We got the Devil. Yeah, we caught him and we got him all tied up down in the basement. Yes, we do. But he ain't so tied up that he can't get loose and get to you, Brother Jonah."

That jarred Brother Jonah out of his daydream and got his attention real good, which encouraged the preacher, so he got even more wound up. "Oh yes, brothers and sisters, we sure have caught old Devil and we got him tied up down in the basement. Yes, we do. But he ain't so tied up that he can't get loose and get to you, Sister Mary Ann, if you ain't careful."

Sister Mary Ann sat up and squirmed in her seat. Oh, the preacher had the whole congregation under his control—that is, all except for three little boys poking at each other about four rows back. Preacher thought he'd try it one more time, so he said, "Oh yes, boys and girls, it's gonna be a great week, I know it is, because we've got the Devil all tied up down in the basement. Yes, we do. But he ain't so tied up that he can't get loose and get to you, Billy Thompson, if you ain't careful."

At that, little Billy stood up and said, "Well, preacher, if you can't tie him up no better than that you might just as well turn him loose."

—*Wood Newton*

The Preacher's Donkey

A preacher wanted to raise money for his church, and, being told there was a fortune in horse racing, he decided to purchase one and race him. However, at the auction the going price for horses was so steep he ended up buying a donkey instead. He figured that since he had the donkey, he might as well go ahead and enter it in the races. To his surprise, the donkey came in third.

The next day, the racing form carried this headline: "Preacher's Ass Shows."

The preacher was so pleased with the donkey he entered it in the races again, and this time it won. The form said, "Preacher's Ass Out In Front."

The bishop was so upset with this kind of publicity, he ordered the preacher not to enter the donkey in any more races. The newspaper printed this headline: "Bishop Scratches Preacher's Ass."

This was just too much for the bishop. He ordered the preacher to get rid of the animal. The preacher decided to give it to a nun in a nearby convent. The headline the next day was, "Nun Has Best Ass In Town." The bishop fainted.

The next day, the bishop informed the nun that she would have to dispose of the donkey, so she finally found a farmer who was willing to buy it for ten dollars. The paper stated: "Nun Peddles Ass For Ten Bucks."

They buried the bishop the next day.

—*Charley Pride*

God's Gonna Take Care of Me

Let me tell you a story about a flood in the Delta country. Civil defense folks pulled up to the front porch and there sat a farmer. The water was done up over his boots. The civil defense man in the boat said, "Oh, sir, it's projected and predicted that the dam is about to bust. Get in the boat. Let me save you."

He said, "You go ahead, fellow, with your boat. God's gonna take care of me."

Five hours later, the boat came back and the fellow was sitting up on the roof, hanging onto the chimney. Water was up over his belt buckle. The civil defense boat pulled up and the man said, "Oh, sir, get in the boat. The dam did bust. Ain't no hope for you. Get in the boat."

The man said, "Y'all go ahead. God's gonna take care of me."

About an hour later, a helicopter flew over. The man is standing up on the chimney. That helicopter hovered down over him, and let the rope down. They had a bullhorn. "Catch a-hold of the rope, sir! This is your last chance. Catch a-hold of the rope."

The fellow said, "Go ahead. God's gonna take care of me."

Well, the scene shifts to heaven. The fellow is graveyard dead—drowned. The fellow looked at the Lord and said, "Lord, I'm disappointed. You said you was going to take care of me. I'm embarrassed."

The Lord said, "You dummy, I sent you two boats and a helicopter!"

—Jerry Clower

He Looked Like Conway

A small town church hired a new preacher. Young, good looking, and fresh out of seminary, the preacher decided it would be a good idea to get out into the community and get acquainted with his congregation.

At the first house, when the lady opened the door, she exclaimed, "My goodness, it's Conway Twitty!"

"No, ma'am, I'm your new minister," he said. "But thanks for the compliment. He's a very fine singer."

"Well, you sure look like Conway," she replied, inviting him in for tea with her family.

As the preacher made his rounds, it seemed that almost every time he knocked he got the same greeting, "My-my, it's Conway Twitty!" And he had to tell them who he really was. Sometimes they didn't believe him at first, his likeness to Twitty was so uncanny, so he had to convince them he really was the new preacher.

Finally, he came to a house where the lady of the house was just drying off from taking a shower. This lady had just talked to a girlfriend on the phone, inviting her to come right over, so when she heard the knock she assumed it was her friend. She threw a towel around her neck and ran to the door. When she opened it, she was startled. She said, "Why, it's Conway Twitty."

The preacher smiled, said, "Hello, Darlin'," and stepped inside.

—*Steve Wariner*

A Great Religious Moment

A little boy was drawing a picture in Sunday School. The teacher asked, "Tell me, what are you drawing?"

"God," the little boy said.

"Well," the teacher said, "nobody really knows what God looks like."

"They will in a minute," replied the boy.

—*Jim Stafford*

Good News and Bad News

"My daughter changed her major from religion and philosophy to geography. When my wife told one of her former teachers about it, he remarked, 'Well, at least she'll always know where she is–she just won't know why.'"

—*Billy Edd Wheeler*

Show Business

Janis Ian

❝ That's not a good song—it just sounds like one! **❞**

—*Richard Leigh,*
quoting Paul Craft's response
to a song he'd just heard

The Demo Was Different

A Nashville musician dies and goes to heaven. When Saint Peter greets him at the Pearly Gates he says, "My son, welcome to heaven. Now, it's my duty to show you around, to make sure you like it here and want to stay." So Saint Peter takes the musician on a tour of heaven, shows him streets of gold, lovely Elysian Fields, where he hears angels singing in heavenly harmony. It was beautiful. It was nice.

Then Saint Peter says, "Well, my son, this is heaven. Now, it's my duty to tell you about your other options." He takes out a cassette player and says, "Let me play you this tape." On the tape there's a wild party going on, like it's New Orleans during Mardi Gras. Bands are playing, people are singing, laughing and having a wonderful time. The musician's eyes light up and he says, "Ah, Saint Peter, that's for me. I gotta go for that."

Boom! Next thing you know, the guy's in a deep, dark pit in hell. People are crying and moaning, rolling around in hot grease, sticking each other with pitchforks, fighting and sweating in anger and pain. It's a bad scene, totally. The musician spies the Devil over in the corner, so he runs up to him and says, "Hey, man, what's the deal here? This is not like the tape that Saint Peter played for me."

The Devil just smiles at him and says, "It's a hell of a demo, isn't it?"

—Jay Vern

How You Get There

This guy was walking along the sidewalk in Nashville. He had a guitar slung over his shoulder, one of ten thousand just like him who make it to Nashville with stars in their eyes, hoping to find fame and fortune in the music business.

A car pulls up beside him and a tourist yells out through the window, "Hey, buddy, can you tell us how you get to the Country Music Hall of Fame?"

"Yeah," he says, "practice till you're dead!"

—*Mickey Newbury*

Three Doors to Heaven

A doctor, a lawyer, and a musician die at the same time and meet at the Pearly Gates. The doctor goes up to Saint Peter and asks what he has to do to get into heaven. Saint Peter says, "Go down the hallway there and take the third door on the right. That's where the doctors go into heaven." The doctor thanks him and walks away.

The lawyer approaches Saint Peter and asks the same question. Saint Peter says, "Go down the hallway and take the second door on the left. That's where the lawyers go into heaven." The lawyer thanks him and hurries down the hall.

The musician asks Saint Peter what he has to do to get into heaven. Saint Peter says, "Well, you go down this hallway and turn left at the kitchen—"

—*Jay Vern*

Music in the Morgue

A medical student was in the morgue one day after classes, getting in a little practice before the upcoming final exams.

He went over to a table where a body was lying face down. He removed the sheet over the body and to his surprise found a cork in the corpse's rectum. Figuring this was fairly unusual, he pulled the cork out and to his surprise music began playing, and a voice sang, "On the road again, I just can't wait to get on the road again."

The student was amazed. He placed the cork back in the rectum and the music stopped. Totally freaked out, he called the medical examiner over to the corpse. "Look at this," he said, "this is really something." He pulled the cork out again and, sure enough, here came the music: "On the road again, I just can't wait to get on the road again."

"So what?" the medical examiner said, obviously unimpressed with the student's discovery.

"But isn't that the most incredible thing you've ever seen?" the student asked.

"Are you kidding?" replied the examiner. "Any asshole can sing country music."

—*John D. Loudermilk*

Delayed Reaction

There was a songwriter who had been on rough times, sort of, but he was also an amateur magician. So he went to an amateur night at a showplace for magicians, hoping to get another occupation going that he could fall back on.

When it got to be his time to take the stage, he mustered up all his courage and, affecting a razzle-dazzle showbiz style, called for a volunteer from the audience.

A man came up and our songwriter magician said, "Now, I'm going to hand you this sledgehammer, and I'm going to place my head on this Bricko-block. And when my head is on the block, I want you to hit me as hard as you can, okay?"

The man nodded, accepted the sledgehammer, and when the magician placed his head on the block, he hit him hard, just as he'd been instructed.

A Jolly-Jolly Funeral Song

This is a true story as it was told to me by Dennis Wilson, who sings backup for a lot of people in Nashville. A friend of his sings at funerals and weddings, and this guy got a call from a lady whose husband had died of a heart attack. She said, "I heard you sing at my cousin's funeral, and I wondered if you'd sing at my husband's funeral, who just died?"

The guy said, "Yes, ma'am, that's what I do. Did you have anything particular in mind?"

She said, "Well, it was so sudden and I'm so upset, I haven't been able to think straight."

"What was something he really liked?" the guy asked, and she finally thought long enough about it to come up with "Jingle Bells."

"Yes, that's it," she said. "He really liked 'Jingle Bells.' Maybe you could sing that one."

The guy said, "'Jingle Bells' wouldn't be appropriate for a funeral, would it?"

"But that was his favorite song," the woman insisted.

"Okay, then," he said, "I'll do it."

When he got there, everybody was crying and carrying on— it had been such a sudden death—but he got up and started singing, "Dashing through the snow . . . " People started frowning and giving him dirty looks. He could feel the hostility in the air. But he managed to finish the song and sit back down.

After the funeral, the lady comes over with the money to pay him for singing. As she handed him the envelope she said in a scolding voice, "I meant 'Glory Bells'!"

—**Bobby Braddock** 🌹

Five years later, the magician comes out of the coma and says, "Ta-da!"

—*Wayland Holyfield* 🌹

Withholding Critical Information

I went over to see my friend the other day, who's a bass player, and I heard this horrible racket behind the front door, a really loud commotion. When he started to open the door it was still going on; I heard more yelling and scuffling.

He stepped outside and I asked him what was wrong. He said, "Well, one of my sons detuned one of my bass strings, and it made me so mad I've been beating the dickens out of him."

"What's the problem?" I asked.

He said, "He won't tell which one it was."

—*Randy Goodrum* 🌹

High-Class Hotels

Me and Bob, here [Bobby Clark, his mandolin player] travel around in the winter months doing conventions—that's when the fairs and bluegrass festivals are kinda calmed down—and these conventions are high-carpet deals. They fly you around and put you up in high-class hotels.

Now, I've only stayed in one first-class hotel. That was up in Virginia. We'as up there doing a show, and later after the show, it was about three o'clock in the morning, I was laying in bed there asleep. Boy, was I tired, and I was just a-snoring away when a knock come on the door.

It scared me. I sat up in bed. I said, "Who is it?"

Short Takes from Bruce Burch

In the dog-eat-dog world of music publishing, the songwriter is the last link on the food chain. Which might explain why a songwriter might approach a hot recording artist, known to occasionally cross a T or dot an I, and say, "Hey man, listen to this new song you and I just wrote!"

Q: What do you call a songwriter without a girlfriend?
A: Homeless.

Someone asked a songwriter, "How do you make a small fortune in the music business?" The songwriter scratched his head and replied, "Start with a large fortune."

A songwriter won the lottery, so the local newspaper sent a reporter to interview him. The reporter's first question was, "What do you plan to do with all that money?" To which the songwriter replied: "Just keep on writing songs until it's all gone."

An old songwriter was sitting at the bar enjoying his drink, when a sexy-looking young lady approached him and said, "Hey, dude, it's your lucky night. Some of your writing buddies got together and enlisted me to come and offer you super sex." The old man looked her over appreciatively, but said, "Honey, at my age, if it's all the same to you, I'll just take the soup!"

—Bruce Burch

This big ol' gruff voice outside said, kinda low like, "Have you got a woman in there with you?"

I said, "No, sir."

Well, he opened up the door and throwed one in!

Now, that's a first-class hotel. (But I made her leave, Sweetie.)

—Mike Snider

"Hokey Pokey" Creator Dies

March 15, 2001: I don't usually pass on sad news like this, but sometimes we need to pause and remember what life is about. There was a great loss recently in the entertainment world. Larry LaPrise, the Detroit native who wrote the song "Hokey Pokey," died last week at eighty-three.

It was especially difficult for the family to keep him in his casket. They'd put his left leg in, and . . . well, you know the rest.

—Bonnie Taggert

Educated Bed Bugs

We don't always get to stay in them nice hotels like that. Lots of times when we're traveling and have to spend the night, I have to pay the bill, so we don't stay in the fancy ones. We stay in better ones than we used to, though, 'cause I got broke from that habit one night. We pulled in this place and I saw it on the sign: DOUBLE ROOMS, $19.95. I thought, boy, I'm gonna get out cheap here.

So I pulled in there. The office looked pretty clean, so I'as signing our name up, and I noticed a bed bug crawling across the page where I'as signing us in. I thought, now I've seen some awful smart bed bugs, but I ain't never seen one that come down to see which room I was checking into!

I got the key and went on up to the room. Got the Presidential Suite that night. Least, I thought it was. It had peanut shells and jellybeans laying all over the floor, like Jimmy Carter and Ronald Reagan might have been there.

This motel was so cheap, the smoke alarms was coin-operated.

When I went to get in the shower, I had to squeeze in it. Had a little narrow door. You could just barely squeeze in and barely squeeze out.

Has any of y'all ever backed out of a hot shower square into a cold doorknob? With the key still in it?

A knock come on the door and a voice said, "It's the maid." I said, "Lady, whatever you do, don't turn that doorknob!"

—*Mike Snider*

Dangerous Environment for Banjo Jokes

A guy walked into a bar and said to the bartender, "Hey, I've got this great banjo player joke. Would you li—"

"Wait a minute, buddy," the bartender said. "Hold on. Before you tell this joke—do you see that wiry, ornery-looking scutter at the end of the bar with the Harley Davidson tattoos? That's my pappy, and he plays the banjo. And do you see that hombre at the other end of the bar, with the scars across his face? Those are his boxing trophies yonder. He's my cousin, and he plays the banjo. And do you see that mangy mongrel in the corner, who looks like me, but is bigger and meaner-looking? That's my brother, and he plays the banjo. Now, are you sure you want to tell that banjo player joke?"

"Well, hell no," the guy said. "Not if I have to explain it three times!"

—*Muriel Anderson*

Work and Play

Paul Craft

66 My mother never did understand what I did for a living. I'm sure she died thinking, 'I wish Paul would quit writing those songs and get a job.' 99

—*Paul Craft*

Bill Monroe and Old Blue Eyes

When they moved the famed Bing Crosby Golf Tournament from California to Winston-Salem, North Carolina, Frank Sinatra happened to be entertaining there at the same time as Bill Monroe. Frank told the tournament's organizers he'd like to meet the "Father of Bluegrass," so they got hold of Bill and led him into the presence of His Pop Music Majesty. "Mr. Monroe," Frank said, "I just want you to know I'm aware of your great contribution to American music, and it's a pleasure to meet you."

They shook hands. And then Bill said to Frank Sinatra, "And what do you do?"

—Chet Atkins, CGP

A Friend of Bill Gates

A man was in the airport in Washington, D.C., waiting for a client who was supposed to meet him there for a business consultation. While he was waiting for his client's flight to arrive, he looked across the waiting area and spotted Bill Gates. He sat there for a while, and then he thought to himself, "Well, heck, I'll just walk over there and say hello."

So he walked up to Bill Gates and said, "Excuse me, Mr. Gates, but I'm a great admirer of yours. I admire what you've done, and all the things you've accomplished and, uh—my name's Chris."

Bill Gates said, "Nice to meet you, Chris."

Encouraged by Gates's friendliness, the man said, "Would you do me a small personal favor? I've got a client coming in on the next plane—we're doing some business together—so, when you see me and him over there talking, after a few minutes, would you mind walking over and saying, 'Hi, Chris, how're you doing?' I mean, he's a good client and it would really impress him."

Gates said, "Why, I'd be glad to."

The man's client finally arrived, and they sat and talked for three or four minutes. Then, Bill Gates casually walked over and tapped him on the shoulder. He said, "Hello, Chris, how's it going?"

The man looked up and said, "Buzz off, Gates, I'm in a meeting!"

—Glenn Sutton 🌹

Woman in the Wet Suit

For ten years he had been stranded on the small desert island. Then one day he spies a dot on the horizon. He stares at it. It gets bigger and bigger until it walks out of the waves toward him taking off its skin-tight cap and shaking out a full head of raven hair—a beautiful, voluptuous woman in a wet suit. She asks, "How long has it been since you had a cigarette?" He says, "Ten years." She unzips a pocket, lights a cig and hands it to him.

"How long since you had a drink?" Again he replies, "Ten years." She unzips another pocket and hands him a miniature bottle of bourbon.

Then she smiles seductively and begins unzipping her wet suit. "And how long has it been since you played around?"

The man's eyes light up and he says, "Honey, if you pull a set of golf clubs out of there—I've died and gone to heaven!"

—Jerry Reed

He Made an Asset of His Handicap

This nice young man had a stuttering problem. But he managed to get a job selling Bibles, and on his first day out he sold ten Bibles.

This made his employer very happy. "Wow, you went out and sold ten Bibles your first day? I'm thrilled, son, really thrilled," the employer said. "So tomorrow I'm giving you twenty Bibles."

The young man went out the next day and sold all twenty Bibles. His boss was so carried away he just had to ask, "Son, how on earth did you manage to sell twenty Bibles?"

The young man said, "Well, I j-j-just ask t-them if they w-w-want to b-buy a Bible, or do t-t-they want me to r-r-read it to th-them?"

—Eddy Arnold

Somewhere Out of Sight

A proctologist went into a bank to cash a check. When he reached into his shirt pocket for something to write with, he pulled out a rectal thermometer. "Hmmm," he muttered. "I wonder where I left my pen?"

—Jack "Cowboy" Clement

A Golf Shot He Remembered

A man was playing a round of golf with his wife on a brand new course, when his drive sliced to the right and ended up in the rough behind an old barn that hadn't yet been removed. Seeing him take out an iron, his wife rushed over and asked what he was doing. He said, "I thought I'd use this pitching wedge and chip the ball back into the fairway."

"Don't be silly," she said. "Look, the barn doors are wide open. Take your 3-wood and hit straight for the green. You might par the hole." He nodded and took out his 3-wood. The shot he hit was fabulous and looked like it was sailing through the barn without any trouble. But at the last second it struck a beam, zoomed back like a bullet, beaned his wife on the side of her head and killed her.

A few weeks later, he was playing golf again and happened to slice the ball to the exact same spot, in the rough behind the barn. When he took out his pitching wedge, his playing partner rushed up and said, "Don't be silly, man. Look, the barn doors are wide open. Plenty room there to hit a 3-wood to the green and save par."

"Huh-uh," the man said sadly. "The last time I tried that I had to take a bogey on this hole!"

—Floyd Cramer

Salesman Johnny

Johnny was a senior in high school and spending the summer with his uncle in Texas. He asked his uncle about finding work. "Well, we've got the biggest store in the world right here," the uncle boasted. "They sell everything under the sun, so it'd be a good place to start. They're always advertising for salesmen. You reckon you could cut the mustard?"

"I reckon I could try," Johnny said modestly. So the uncle, who knew the boss at the store, sent him in for an interview.

The boss looked Johnny over and asked, "Have you ever been a salesman before?"

"Yes sir, I did a little selling last summer."

"What did you sell?"

"Bibles," Johnny said with a twinkle in his eye. "I'd stutter real bad when I introduced myself, and then I'd say, 'Y-y-you want to buy a B-Bible, or c-could I read some of it f-fo-for you?' I sold about fifteen hundred Bibles, I reckon."

"Uh-huh," the boss said skeptically. But he had taken a liking to Johnny. "All right, I'll try you out. Come in tomorrow and report to our marine department. I'll check on you at the end of the day, to see how you made out. Think you could sell fishing equipment and such?"

"I reckon I could try," Johnny said.

The next day proved to be a busy one for salesman Johnny, and he was really tired by the time five o'clock rolled around. Pretty soon the boss showed up and said, "You look done-in, boy. How many customers did you wait on today?"

"One, sir."

"Only one?" The boss was very disappointed. "And taking care of just one customer wore you out?" Johnny nodded. "Well, how much did you take in?"

"Exactly one hundred and one thousand, three hundred thirty-four dollars and fifty-three cents," Johnny said, grinning shyly.

The boss was flabbergasted. "How did you manage that, son?"

"Well, sir, this man came in and I sold him a small fish hook, then a medium fish hook, and finally a really large hook. Then I sold him a small rod and reel, a medium rod and reel, and a great big rod and reel. I asked him where he was going fishing, and he said maybe down the coast, so I told him he'd probably need a fishing boat. I took him to our boat department and sold him that fancy twenty-two foot Chris Craft with twin engines. Then he said his Honda Civic probably wouldn't be able to handle the load, so I took him to the vehicle department and sold him a new GMC one-ton pickup truck."

"You sold all that to a guy who came in to buy a fish hook?" the boss asked in astonishment.

"He didn't come in to buy a fish hook, sir," Johnny explained. "He came in to buy a box of tampons for his wife. So I said to him, 'Your weekend's shot. Maybe you ought to think about going fishing.'"

—*Faron Young*

He Drove to Heaven

This guy went out to play a round of golf, and he was feeling really good. He reached in his bag and took out his driver, teed the ball up on the first tee, took a mighty swing, and hit the ball right in the screws. He looked up to watch it sail three hundred and twenty-five yards down the fairway.

Just as it finished its roll, though, it tailed off and ended up in the woods. But he did not care. He was happy. He went dancing down the fairway and skip-hopped into the woods to look for the ball. He found it in a place so dense with trees, only a small hole appeared in the leaves above, a hole about the size of a number three washtub.

He still felt good. He was so confident, he said to himself, "The way I'm hitting it today, I can take an iron and smack the ball right through the middle of that hole up there." So he selected his iron and took a strong, full swing at it. The ball flew up, hit a tree trunk, and shot back at him like a bullet. It whacked him on the side of the head and killed him dead. *Whonk!*

When he woke up, Saint Peter was sitting there shaking him. Saint Peter said, "Boy, am I glad to see you. We need a foursome tomorrow, and it's for the tournament championship. I heard you're really into golf. Are you pretty good?"

The guy looked at him and smiled. "Well, I got here in two!"

—Red Lane 🌹

Mud for the Soul

After being told by several legitimate doctors that he probably ought not be thinking about making long-term investments, this man went to see a different sort of doctor. If you wanted to flatter him, you might call him a quack.

"Doc," he said to the quack, "I been told I ain't got much time left on this old earth ball. So, right now you're my doctor of choice. What can you do for me?"

The doctor gave him a thorough examination and asked him questions about his medical history, acting very professional and concerned. The man began to have hope, thinking this doctor might not be such a quack, after all.

Finally, the doctor said, "My professional instincts, coupled with my gut feeling, tells me we need to schedule you for a series of mud baths."

"Ah," the man said smiling, "that sounds good to me. And, Doctor, do you think that by taking all these mud baths, it will draw the sickness out of me, and I'll be okay?"

"No," the doctor replied. "But it will get you used to the dirt!"

—*David Ball*

The Genie

A couple was golfing one day on a very exclusive course, lined with million-dollar houses. On the third tee, the husband said, "Honey, be careful when you drive the ball, and don't knock out any windows. It could cost us a fortune."

The wife teed up, and shanked the ball right through the picture window of the largest house on the course. The husband cringed. "All right," he said, "let's go apologize and see what this is going to cost." They knocked on the door, and heard a voice inviting them to come in. Inside, they saw glass all over the floor, and a broken bottle lying on its side in the foyer.

A man on the couch said, "Are you the people who broke the window?" The husband nodded, and said he was sorry. "No, actually, I want to thank you," the man said. "I'm a genie, and I've been trapped in that bottle for a thousand years. You've released me. And now I'm allowed to grant three wishes. I'll give you each a wish, and keep the last one for myself."

"Great!" said the husband. "I want a million dollars a year for the rest of my life."

"No problem," said the genie. "It's done." He looked at the wife. "And what is your wish?"

"I want a house in every country of the world," she said, and the genie said it was done.

The husband said, "Now, genie, what is your wish?"

"Well, since I've been trapped in that bottle, I haven't been with a woman for a thousand years. My wish is to sleep with your wife."

The husband looked at his wife and said, "Well, we did get a lot of money, and all those houses, honey. I guess I don't care, if you don't."

So the genie took the wife upstairs. After it was over, the genie rolled aside, looked at the wife and said, "How old is your husband?"

"Thirty-five," she replied.

"And he still believes in genies? That's amazing!"

—Joe Taggert

Rural Life

Merle Travis

" These old country stores, they're great places to set around and chew tobacco and whittle and play checkers and run down your neighbor's character. "

—*James Still*

Bill Monroe and Mike Snider

Bill was pitching one of his songs to Opry star Mike Snider, really laying it on thick, saying, "You ought to record this song, Mike, it's powerful. Powerful. It's a great song and it'd be perfect for you."

When Bill told him the name of the song, Mike said, "Well, Bill, I've heard that song, and I don't like it."

Bill's famous temper flared up at that. He said, "Well, that song don't like you neither, and you ain't no part a-nothing!"

—*Chet Atkins, CGP*

A Place in the Country

People are always talking about going to the country these days. I have an old uncle who lives out in the hills of Kentucky. I went out there to see him. I drove my car on the blacktop as far as it went, then took a graveled road and then a dirt road. I had to hire a mule and wagon, and when the road ran out, I unhitched the mule and rode it for a while. Finally, I had to swing across the creek on a grapevine to get to my uncle's house, and when I got there I found a note on the door that said, "Gone to the country for the weekend."

—Grandpa Jones

Last Move for the Old Outhouse

A Texas farmer was approached by representatives of a large oil company, who told him their soundings in the area indicated there might be oil on his land. They said he could become rich, so he gave them permission to do exploratory drilling with their giant auger.

They went down through topsoil, clay, shale, limestone, and other layers of substrata for over two hundred feet, but didn't strike oil. So they reported this to him and started making preparations to fill in and cover the large hole in the ground they'd made.

That's when the farmer got an idea. He said, "Say, if you don't mind, instead of capping it off how's about taking your crane and lifting that outhouse from where it's at and setting it down over that hole. I'll never have to move it again."

So with some misgivings, they did just that.

The morning after the outhouse was relocated, the farmer's grandson came running up to the house in a fit of agitation. "Papaw, Papaw," he cried out, "I was walking by the outhouse, and since the door was part-way open, I saw Granny sitting in there and she looked terrible. Her eyes were crossed and she was red-white-and-blue in the face. I'm afraid she's dying."

"Now, son," the farmer said unconcerned, "don't fret. Your grandma will be all right. She just likes to hold her breath 'til she hears it hit bottom!"

—Grandpa Jones

El Roho

Farmer Redmon had about two hundred hens, but his roosters were over the hill and not getting the job done, and he wanted chicks. So he advertised for a virile rooster.

He soon got a call from a farmer not too far away who said he had the world's most sexually active rooster. His name was El Roho, and the price was $1500.

Farmer Redmon thought the price was high, but if El Roho was really that good, he'd be worth it. So he bought him.

He took El Roho back to his farm and set him down in the middle of the barnyard, then gave him a pep talk. "Now, El Roho, there's a lot of hens to service here, so take your time. I want you to do a good job and have fun, but you cost me a lot of money, so for goodness sakes, pace yourself."

The rooster seemed to understand. Mr. Redmon pointed him toward the henhouse, and El Roho took off like a shot. Wham-wham-wham, he nailed every hen there—a few of them twice. After that, he heard a commotion in the duck pen. Sure enough, El Roho was there, topping every single duck. Farmer Redmon was shocked. He'd never seen a performance like that, and as proud as he was, he was afraid El Roho would wear himself out.

But El Roho acted like he was just warming up. He ran to the pond and nailed a gaggle of geese, came back to the house and jumped two cats, three dogs, and knocked off a row of cabbages as he left the premises. The last time Redmon saw him he was out in the fields chasing quail and pheasants until the sun went down. He had a sinking feeling he would never see El Roho alive again.

Redmon went to bed and just as he'd figured, the next morning he saw El Roho lying on his back out in the meadow, with a circle of buzzards overhead. He looked to be stone cold dead. "I reckon he's loved himself to death," Redmon thought.

Saddened by the loss of such an expensive and colorful animal, he walked out to him and said, "Oh, El Roho, I told you to pace yourself, and now look at you. Well, come on, I'll take you back and bury you."

As he bent down he was startled to see one of El Roho's eyes open. The rooster winked at him, nodded up toward the buzzards, and said, "Shhhh, they're getting closer."

—*Norman Gimbel*

A Helpful Reminder

This old boy rode his mule to a pie supper. Halfway through the meal, he went out to check on him and found that somebody'd painted his tail red. Man, was he mad. He went back inside and said, "All right, will the wise guy what painted my mule's tail red stand up right now."

This big hulky Okie stood up—looked to be seven feet tall—and his knuckles still drug the ground. He said, "I'm your man. What about it?" The mule owner smiled at him and said, "I just wanted to let you know—that first coat's dry."

—*Roger Miller* 🌹

The Son Went to Ohio

A barber asked one of his customers how his son was doing. The man said his son had gone up to Ohio and got a job making pretty good money. The barber asked him whereabouts in Ohio. The man said, "Why, right downtown!"

—*Merle Travis*

Marcel and the City Fella

One day, me and Marcel Ledbetter was laying by a patch of corn. We had throwed some whippoorwill peas down in the water furrow, where that old Sutton spring-tooth harrow would roll them peas around. They would come up and we could have us some fall peas to eat. This fellow come driving up in one of them A-model cars. He jumped out and said, "Hey, boy."

Marcel said, "You talking to me?"

He said, "Yeah."

Marcel said, "Whoa, Della. What you want, city fella?"

He said, "Those rows you plowing here, they sure are crooked."

Marcel Ledbetter said, "You can grow just as much corn on a crooked row as you can on a straight one."

The fellow said, "Well, the corn shore is yellow."

Marcel said, "We planted yellow corn."

The fellow said, "Well, there ain't very much between you and a fool, is it?"

Marcel said, "Nothing but a fence."

—*Jerry Clower*

A Blushing Bit of Bullish Bickering

A man and woman went to a cattle auction. There were three top bulls auctioned off that day. After the sale, the woman approached the auctioneer and asked, "How many times a year would that third-most expensive bull be active?"

The auctioneer said, "Well, I would guess about fifty times."

The woman turned to her husband and said, "See?"

Then she asked, "How many times a year would that second-most expensive bull be active?"

The auctioneer said he thought it would be about seventy-five times. Again the woman turned to her husband and said, "See?"

Then she pointed to the highest-priced bull and asked, "Okay, and how many times a year would that pretty boy be active?" The man said he would guess, oh, about a hundred times. The woman smiled and looked at her husband yet again, saying even more forcefully, "See?"

The husband said to the auctioneer, "Would all of those times be with the same cow?"

"Of course not," the auctioneer said.

The husband turned to his wife and said, "See?"

—Jim Stafford

Out to See the World

This guy lived so far back in the hollows near Drakesboro, Kentucky, he had never been to a town of any size, much less a city, but he got to thinking he'd like to get out and see the world. A man who lived near him was a coal truck driver, so he started bugging the man to take him with him on a trip. The man said he'd do it, but he kept putting him off. He'd tell the guy to meet him at the truck at 9:00 the next morning, then drive off at 8:30. Next time, he'd tell the guy to be there at 7:30, and he'd leave at 7:00.

This went on until the poor guy caught on and showed up early one morning, so the man had to take him along. In the first town they came to, the man stopped his truck at a traffic light. It surprised his passenger, who asked him what was wrong. Why was he stopping? The man pointed up and said, "That red light up there."

The guy leaned out of the cab window and looked up at the light. Then he yelled back at the man and motioned with his inside hand. "Come on," he said, "you're gonna miss it by a good two feet!"

—Merle Travis

The Home Front

*Vince Gill &
Billy Edd
Wheeler*

66 Marriage is a fifty-fifty proposition.
The men tell us what to do, and we
tell them where to go. 99

—*Minnie Pearl*

The Amazing Sausage Machine

A nice gentleman dedicated his entire life to perfecting a sausage machine that was nothing short of a miracle. It made him millions. He had married late in life, and so had a son in his thirties who had not really grown up emotionally. The son had smoked a lot of wacky weed and was what you'd call a modern-day hippie.

Still, he was the old man's only son, and although he'd never shown any interest in Dad's business, he stood to inherit the family fortune. Dad had never given up on him. He thought if he could get the "boy" to come and walk through his sausage factory with him as he explained the intricate workings of it, they might yet bond and Dad could one day die in peace.

When the day came, the son arrived in the slouchiest clothes imaginable, a tank top which allowed his colorful and flowery tattoos to shine, ragged pants, and beat-up sandals. His hair was three different bright colors.

The father overlooked all that and proceeded to lead his son through the factory, proudly pointing out every facet of the business. At every turn, the son's response was, "Ho-hum," or "Big deal," or "Is that it, that's all there is to it?"

Finally the man came to the culmination of his life's work—a gleaming, stainless-steel affair he looked at with admiration. "Son," he said with pride, "this is my amazing sausage machine. You see, you put the live pig in here, and the sausage comes out there. What do you think of that?"

The boy yawned and said, "Big deal. But, hey, show me a machine where you put the sausage in here, and a live pig comes out there . . . I could really dig that, man."

The father said, "Son, I don't have a machine like that. But your mother does!"

—*Jimmy Dean*

No Thanks Needed

A married couple was in a terrible accident where the woman's face was severely burned. The doctor told the husband he couldn't graft any skin from her body because she was too slender, so the husband volunteered to donate some of his own skin. However, the doctor found that the only skin he considered suitable would have to come from the husband's buttocks.

The husband and wife agreed: they would tell no one where the skin came from, and requested that the doctor honor their secret. After all, this was a delicate matter.

After surgery was performed, everyone was astounded at the woman's new beauty. She looked better than she ever had. Her friends and relatives went on and on about her radiance, her youthful beauty. One day when she was alone with her husband, she was overcome with emotion at his sacrifice. She said, "Dear, I want to thank you for everything you did for me. There's no way I could ever repay you."

"Hey, baby," he said smiling, "forget about it. I get all the thanks I need every time I see your mother kiss you on the cheek."

—Archie Campbell

Years of Practice

Roscoe and his buddy Burl were swapping notes on married life. Roscoe said, "My wife and I have been married for twenty years, and she's been throwing things at me ever since we got married. I tell you, Burl, I'm starting to get sick and tired of it."

"After all this time," Burl replied, "why are you complaining about it now?"

Roscoe said, "I'm getting slower, and her aim's getting better!"

—Archie Campbell

Magic at the Mall

A Tennessee timber man from way back in the hills took his boy to visit a mall. They were amazed by almost everything they saw, but especially by two shiny, silver walls that would move apart and then slide back together again.

The boy asked, "What is that, Dad?" But his father had never seen anything like it. He said he didn't know. While the boy and his father were watching in amazement, a fat old lady in a wheelchair rolled up to the moving walls and pressed a button. The walls opened and the lady rolled between them into a small room. The walls closed and the boy and his father watched the small circular numbers above the walls light up in sequence. They continued to watch until it reached the last number, and then the numbers began to light in the reverse order.

Finally the walls opened up again and a gorgeous, voluptuous twenty-four year-old blonde woman stepped out. The father, not taking his eyes off the young woman, said quietly to his son, "Go get your mother."

—*Archie Campbell*

At a Loss for Names

There was this woman who had so many children she ran out of names to call her husband.

—*Minnie Pearl*

Minnie Pearl had so much fun talking about relationships between men and women, I think she would have loved some of these, which might be considered payback for all the blonde jokes guys send out:

Q: How does a man show that he is planning for the future?
A: He buys two cases of beer.

Q: How many men does it take to change a roll of toilet paper?
A: We don't know; it has never happened.

Q: When do you care for a man's company?
A: When he owns it.

Q: What do most men at singles bars have in common?
A: They're married.

Q: Why are married women heavier than single women?
A: Single women come home, see what's in the fridge, and go to bed. Married women come home, see what's in bed, and go to the fridge.

Bubba Loves Kids

I got two boys, Bubba Jr. and Little Bubba. Ain't it amazing how different kids can be and come from exactly the same place? Same gene pool, but one born on the high diving board and one in the shallow end. They are so very different. I put one through college and the other one through a wall!

Maybe it was the way we raised them. Me and Plaintiff—that's what I call my ex-wife—did the best we could. You know how it is when that first child comes along. Everything is new, fresh and clean. We sterilized everything that came within thirty feet of that first baby. He was the cleanest baby that every burped. The second boy came along and, well, he ate with the dog. We have twelve photo albums of the first child. We only got two pictures of the second child, and the neighbors gave us those.

But you gotta love them all. God gave them to us to love, not to understand.

Little Bubba came in one day from second grade and said, "Pop, I'm the smartest kid in my class." I said, "Well, fantastic. Did the teacher tell you that?" He said, "No, I just figured it out all by myself. Do you think I ought to tell the teacher?" I just laughed and said, "No, don't do that, I'm sure she'll figure it out for herself."

—*T. Bubba Bechtol, CSP*

She Had to Whisper

A phone solicitor calls this house and a little girl answers, speaking in a whisper, "Hello."

The caller says, "Why, hi there, little girl, is your mom home?"

"She's busy," she says, still whispering.

The man says, "Oh, I see. Well, all right, is your father there? Let me speak with your father, please."

"He's busy."

"Okay, very good. Is there another adult in the house I could talk with? Do you have someone else there?"

She says, "There's a policeman here."

"A policeman?" The man starts to get worried. "Okay," he says, "let me speak with the policeman."

"He's busy."

"Well, is there anybody else of age there I could talk with?"

"There's a fireman."

"A fireman?" The man is really concerned now. "Listen, young lady," he says, "I'm starting to get very upset here. Now, you tell me right away what's going on there. I want to know what everybody's so busy about, and I want to know right now."

"Sssshhh," she whispers. "They're looking for me!"

—*Mac Davis* 🌹

The Doctor Didn't Like Sauerkraut

A doctor was having an affair with his nurse. A year or so after this started, she told him she was pregnant.

Not wanting his wife to know, he gave the nurse a large sum of money and asked her to go to Germany and have the baby there.

"But how will I let you know the baby is born?" she asked.

"Just send me a postcard," he said, "and write *sauerkraut* on it."

Not knowing what else to do, the nurse took the money and flew to Germany. Six months went by, and then one day the doctor's wife called him at the office and said, "Dear, you received a very strange postcard in the mail today, and I don't understand what it means."

The doctor said, "Just wait until I get home. I'll read it and explain it to you. I'm sure it's nothing important."

Later that evening the doctor came home, read the postcard, and fell to the floor with a heart attack and died. His wife picked up the card and read it again. It said, "Sauerkraut, sauerkraut, sauerkraut, sauerkraut—two with wieners, two without."

—*Bob Jennings*

Info Not in the Census

A census taker went to this one house and knocked on the door. When the woman came out, he asked, "How many children do you have, and what are their ages?"

The woman said, "Well, there are the twins, Sally and Holly. They're eighteen. And the twins, Billie and Willie—they're sixteen. And the twins, Charlie and Jenny, they're fourteen."

"Hold on a minute," the census taker said, a little taken aback. "Let me ask you something—did you get twins every time?"

"Oh my, no," the woman said. "There were hundreds of times when we didn't get anything!"

—*Ralph Emery*

Dreaming the Impossible Dream

A man deep in prayer was walking along a California beach. "Lord," he said, "you have promised to give me what my heart desires. Will you grant my wish? Give me a sign."

Suddenly the clouds parted above him and he heard a booming voice: "I have searched your heart and found it to be pure. The last time I issued a blank request was to Solomon, and he didn't disappoint me. He asked for wisdom. I trust you will follow his example. I will grant you one wish."

The man said at last, "I've always wanted to go to Hawaii, but I'm deathly afraid of flying, and I get seasick on boats. Could you build a bridge to Hawaii so I can drive there for a visit whenever I feel like it?"

The Lord laughed and said, "That's impossible. Think of the logistics. How would the support columns ever reach the bottom of the Pacific? Think how much concrete it would take, how much steel. Your request is very materialistic, and I am disappointed in you. Wish for something higher, something that would honor and glorify Me as well."

The man meditated for a long time. Then he said, "Lord, I've been married and divorced four times. All my wives said I'm not caring. I'm insensitive. I wish I could understand women—know how they feel inside, what they're thinking when they give me the silent treatment, why they're crying, and what they really mean when they shrug and say, 'Nothing.' I want you to reveal to me the true nature of women, and tell me how to make them really happy. That's my wish, Lord."

After a few minutes, God said, "You want two lanes or four on that bridge?"

—*Don Robertson* 🌹

Sixteen Children: The Good News and the Bad

This man and woman, who had twelve kids, decided it was time for them, as a couple, to have their annual check-ups.

After their examinations, the doctor sat them down and said, "Well, you're both very healthy—nothing wrong that I can see. But, I've got some bad news and some good news."

This surprised them, but it also worried them just a little. The husband, deciding to be optimistic, said, "Okay, tell us what the good news is."

The doctor said, "The good news is, your wife's pregnant again."

"Oh, wow," the husband said, "that *is* good news." He gave his wife a big hug. Then he turned and said, "Okay, Doctor—so what's the bad news?"

The doctor said, "The bad news is, she's going to have quadruplets."

"Oh, my goodness," the man said. "That is bad news. We've already got twelve kids, and now, four more. How are we ever going to be able to support four more kids? And furthermore, how in the world are we going to come up with four names for four more kids?"

"I've got a great idea," the doctor said. "Name them, Adolph, Rudolph, Getoff, and Stayoff!"

—Vince Gill

Speaking of babies, I received the following email from Vince Gill's golfing buddy, pro golfer Joe Taggert, on Monday, March 12, 2001, at 4:49 a.m.: "Amy and Vince had a baby girl this morning at 12:36 a.m., weighing in at seven pounds, nine and one-quarter ounces, and is nineteen and a half inches long. No name yet. All family members doing just fine."

The following morning, Joe's email said, "I just got off the phone with Vinny. Still no name for the baby. He said it was tough when you get an Okie and a girl from the Deep South together. Amy wouldn't go for "Augusta," but then she's probably never been to the Masters!"

When I talked to Vince the next day, the 14th, he said they had named the baby Corrina. —Ed.

Stuttering vs. Stammering

Mel Tillis was telling Mickey about being in Chicago when a man approached him and asked how to get to Old Town. Mel could hardly understand the man, he stuttered so badly.

Mel said, "C-can you b-be-believe that? Ain't that f-funny? I just sh-shook my h-head. If I'd answered him, h-he'd a-knocked the h-h-hell out of me, c-cause I stutter too."

Mickey said Mel told him he didn't really stutter, though, he stammered. When he talked in rhythm, or when he sang, he didn't stammer. Mel laughed then, and said, "B-but who in hell w-wa-wants to go around all d-d-day singing?"

—*Mickey Newbury* 🌹

Aging

Sheb Wooley

" My grandmother started walking when she was sixty. She is now ninety-seven, and we don't know where the hell she is!

—Ron Sneed

Six Feet Under in Style

An elderly spinster met with her attorney to discuss her will and the distribution of her assets upon her death. "Besides my furniture and accessories," she revealed, "I have forty thousand dollars in my savings account at the bank."

"How would you like the forty thousand to be distributed?" the lawyer asked.

The spinster said, "Well, I've lived a reclusive life. People have hardly ever noticed me, and I'd like them to notice me when I pass on. I want to provide thirty-five thousand for my funeral."

The lawyer agreed that a thirty-five-thousand-dollar funeral would certainly leave a lasting impression. "What would you like to do with the remaining five thousand?" he asked.

"Well," she replied, "as you know I've never married. I've lived alone almost my entire life and, in fact, I've never slept with a man before. Before I die I'd like to use the five thousand to arrange for a man to sleep with me."

"That's an unusual request," the lawyer said, adding, "but I'll see what I can do to arrange it and get back to you."

That evening, the lawyer told his wife about the eccentric spinster and her weird request. After thinking about how much she could do around the house with five thousand dollars, and with a bit of coaxing, she got her husband to agree to provide the service himself. She said, "I'll drive you over tomorrow morning and wait in the car until you're finished." The next morning she drove him to the spinster's house and waited while he went in. After waiting for over an hour she began to blow the car horn.

Shortly, the upstairs bedroom window opened. Her husband stuck his head out and yelled, "Come back tomorrow. She's decided to let the county bury her!"

—*Bill Anderson* 🌹

Hot Golden Memories

This little old couple was sitting at the table beginning their morning breakfast ritual when the old man said, "Darling, do you remember what we were doing fifty years ago today?"

The cute little lady blushed and said, "Yes. We were on our honeymoon and having breakfast together for the first time as husband and wife."

The man said, "But we were stark naked, remember?"

The lady said, "Yes, I do remember. Hey, let's do it like we did fifty years ago."

They both threw off all their clothes and sat back down to enjoy breakfast.

The old man's eyes twinkled and he said mischievously, "Honey, I have such lovely memories about our honeymoon. Do you as well?"

The cute little old lady blushed shyly and said, "Why yes, I do. In fact, I feel just as hot as I did that very morning."

The little old man looked at his wife and smiled. "Yes, darling," he said, "I suppose you do feel as hot. One boob's hanging in your oatmeal, and one's in your cup of coffee!"

—*Sheb Wooley*

Break the Hex

An old man is playing golf and thinks he hits his ball in the water hazard. He's looking in the marshy part of the hazard for his ball when he sees a little frog staring up at him. The frog says in a squeaky voice, "Help me, help me, pick me up, please." The old man reaches down and picks up the frog, and the frog says, "Ohhhhh, thank you. I'm a magic frog. If you'll turn me over and rub my belly three times I'll turn into a beautiful woman."

The old man smiles, puts the frog in his pocket and resumes looking for his ball. Again he hears a muffled, "Help me, help me!" He reaches back in his pocket and takes out the frog. The frog says, "Didn't you hear me? I said, I'm a magic frog, and if you'll turn me over and rub my belly three times I'll turn into a beautiful woman."

Smiling as he puts the frog back in his pocket, the old man says, "Oh, I heard you all right, but at my age I'd rather have a talking frog!"

—From Ari Dane via Bob Shane

Still Able at Eighty

There's an old couple, both in their eighties, on a sentimental holiday back to the place where they first met. They're sitting in a pub, and he says, "Do you remember the first time we had sex together, over fifty years ago? We went out behind the bar and leaned against the fence."

"Yes," she says, "I remember it well."

"Okay," he says. "How about taking a stroll out there and doing it again, for old time's sake?"

"Oh Henry, you devil, that sounds like a good idea."

There's a man sitting at the next table listening to all this, and he's having a real chuckle. He thinks, "Two old timers making love leaning up against a fence? I've got to see this." So he moves to where he can watch them.

They walk haltingly along, leaning on each other for support, using their walking sticks. Finally they get out behind the bar and make their way to the fence. The old lady turns around and leans against the fence and he moves in. Suddenly they erupt into the most furious lovemaking the man watching has ever seen. They're bucking and jumping like eighteen-year-olds.

This athletic, frenetic love dance goes on for a good twenty minutes until, finally, they both collapse panting on the ground. The guy watching is amazed. He thinks maybe he's learning something about life he didn't know. He wonders if his own aged parents still make love like this.

After lying on the ground recovering for about half an hour, the old man and woman struggle to their feet and get their clothes back in order. As they come into the pub and pass by the guy, he says to the old man, "Sir, that was something else. I can't believe what you two did out there. How do you manage it? What's your secret?"

"Oh, there's no secret," the old man answers. "Except, fifty years ago that confounded fence wasn't electric!"

—Gerry House

The Fastest Thing in the World

These three old guys were sitting around talking, and they got to conjecturing about what was the fastest thing on earth. One said, "It's the blink of an eye." The other two agreed that, yeah, the blink of an eye was fast.

The second man, though, said he thought there was something faster than that: a light switch. "You turn on a light and, bam, you can see it instantly, even if you're a mile away." They agreed that, too, was really fast.

But the third man said, "No-no, a thought is the fastest thing in the world." The other two waited for his explanation. "Last night," he said, "I was lying in bed, when I thought I had to go to the bathroom. Before I could blink an eye or reach for the light— I did!"

—Merle Kilgore 🥀

Thanks but No Thanks

"A young fellow asked me if I'd ever tried Viagra. I told him the truth. Viagra for me would be like putting a brand new flag-pole on a condemned building."

—from Shelly Berman, UCLA,
via Bob Shane

Buddy Killen Remembers Roger Miller 🌹

Buddy Killen was sole owner of Tree Music Publishing Cmpany until he sold it to CBS in 1989. Record producer, author, talent manager, studio owner, etc., Killen was Roger Miller's publisher and friend. Some of his Miller memories:

We were redoing an album of Roger's hits, and the air conditioning wasn't working. He said, "Is it hot in here or is it just my career?"

Roger called one night at 3 A.M. "I'm in jail." I asked him what he did to get arrested. He said, "I was down at Tootsie's and found some florescent light bulbs on the sidewalk, so I started breaking them. The cops pulled up and caught me." I asked why he was breaking the bulbs. He said, "Why, I just wanted to hear 'em pop."

Another time he called and said he had to have three hundred dollars. This was after I'd just bought him a brand new Cadillac. I said, "Roger, you already owe us more than the company's worth, and you haven't written a song in months." He took his guitar into the next room and fifteen minutes later came out with a beautiful song, one called "Home," that went to #1 later as recorded by Jim Reeves. I gave Roger the three hundred and he immediately went out and bought the riding lawn mower he "just had to have," and drove it all the way home from the store, eight miles away!

Humor was so ingrained in Roger, he was joking on his way to the hospital, even when he knew he was dying. He looked out the window at the ocean and said to his wife, "Look, Mary, they've filled our pool!"

Furry and Feathered Friends

*Jack "Cowboy"
Clement*

66 Two camels were walking along in the
desert when one of them said, "I don't
care what anybody says, I'm thirsty. 99

—*Jack "Cowboy" Clement*

Elvis's Monkey

There was an incident one evening involving Elvis's monkey. Actually, I guess it was a chimp, a pet chimp. Anyhow, the chimp was named "Scatter." Guess what he scattered around when he got annoyed? But he was a sweet little guy. When I held him, he would put his arms around my neck. It was like holding a baby.

That same evening, Scatter was allowed to wander around the room for a few minutes. There was a girl sitting across from me. Scatter went over and peeked under her skirt, at which point she let out a little scream and jumped up. Everyone thought it was funny, except the poor girl. (I don't know if you can use this in your book, but I don't think it would offend anyone much, except maybe the chimp's relatives.)

—*Don Robertson*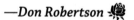

Digging What?

At a U.S. Army base, two soldiers in the field find a dead animal. One says it's a mule, the other says it's a horse. A Colonel breaks up the argument and says, "You're both wrong, it's an ass. Now get your shovels and bury the poor animal."

They're digging away when a nurse comes by and says, "Hi, fellas, are you digging a foxhole?" They say, "Nooooooooo, we're . . ."

—*Bob Shane*

One Was a Talker

Hezzie told me about this man who had some trick dogs, and he put them up for sale. Pretty soon a fellow came down there and asked how much the dogs were going for. The man said he'd let them go for a hundred dollars each. The fellow said that was way too much for dogs, but the owner said, "Huh, you haven't seen what these dogs can do."

He snapped his fingers and the first dog turned a flip and landed on its feet. He snapped his fingers again and the second dog turned a flip and landed on the first dog's back. He snapped his fingers again and the third dog turned a flip, landed on the second dog's back and sang "The Wabash Cannonball."

The fellow was impressed. He said, "I'll take the top one."

The dog owner replied, "You probably wouldn't want to make that choice. It's the middle one that's the ventriloquist."

—*Minnie Pearl*

The Dog Who Went to College

This old gentleman sent his son off to college, gave him four hundred dollars in spending money, told him to study hard and write home often. What he didn't know was his son loved to gamble, and he wasn't too good at it. Wasn't long until the boy got hard up for money, so he dreamed up a scheme to milk some more funds from his dad.

He wrote his father and said, "Dad, I think you'll be interested to know that this college does a lot of experimental work with animals. After I told them about Old Blue, why, they think he'd be a perfect candidate to enter their school for dogs. They think they can teach him to read and write. If you'll send him here on the train, with about five hundred dollars, I'll enroll him in the school."

The old man thought it would be fun to have a dog that could read and write, so he sent Old Blue to his son, along with the five hundred bucks.

It didn't take the boy long to gamble away the money, so he wrote home again and said, "Dad, Old Blue has learned to read and write. He's a whiz. In fact, they think he's a genius. With some more special instruction, what with his IQ and all, they think that for about five hundred more they can teach him to talk."

The boy's father got excited about the prospect of having a dog that could talk, so he mailed the money to his son. As usual, the boy had a streak of bad luck gambling. In about three weeks he was broke again, so he wrote his father and said, "Dad, Old Blue is doing so well with his talking they've got him reading dog books, which they're taping and sending out to institutes of higher learning. All the TV and radio networks are interested in interviewing him. The college is so elated they want to enroll him in their music school. They're positive they can teach him to sing. Please send another five hundred dollars."

The father was beside himself, and quickly sent another five big ones. By the time the boy was supposed to bring Old Blue home for Christmas, Dad had boasted all around about his wonder dog that could talk and sing. The whole county turned out with him to meet the train. When his son stepped off the train, the father ran to him and said, "Son, where's Old Blue?"

"Dad," the boy said grimly, "wait till we get in the pickup and I'll tell you all about it."

"But, son," the father protested, "everybody wants to see Old Blue. Just look, your aunts and uncles are here, your cousins, all our neighbors, the mayor, the newspaper and radio people. Where's Old Blue?"

"I'll tell you when we get in the pickup. Come on."

When they were alone in the pickup, the father said, "All right, let's have it."

"Well," the boy began, "you won't believe how well Old Blue was doing with his reading and writing, and his talking and singing. I couldn't wait for you to hear him. But this morning while I was shaving and getting ready to leave, Old Blue was sitting on the john reading *The Wall Street Journal* and humming 'The Yellow Rose of Texas.' Then all of a sudden he stopped humming, put down the paper and looked up at me. He said, 'Do you reckon your old man is still fooling around with that young school teacher?'

"I tell you, Dad, it made me so mad I took that razor and cut Old Blue's throat."

The old man's face relaxed, and he said, "Are you right sure he's dead?"

—*Jim Reeves*

Jesus Is Watching You

This poor guy decided he wanted to be a burglar. He bought some tools of the trade and one night found a nice house in a nice neighborhood. The house was dark. He thought the owners were probably away, so it would be a good place to start. He managed to open the basement door, turned on his flashlight, and started climbing the stairs.

At the top of the stairs he opened the kitchen door and stepped in. Just then he heard a voice say, "Jesus is watching you." He froze in his tracks. He waited a few minutes in the dark and, hearing nothing more, started to take another step. "Jesus is watching you," came the voice, and again he froze. He was beginning to sweat. The third time he heard the voice, he got up enough nerve to shine the light in the direction it came from. There in a cage above the sink sat a large parrot.

He breathed a sigh of relief, walked to the parrot and said, "You little green idiot. You don't know what you're talking about." Just then he heard a menacing, low-rumbling growl, and swung his light toward the hallway where it came to rest on the red eyes and white bared teeth of a large Doberman.

The parrot said, "Sic him, Jesus!"

—Johnny Russell

The Dead Cat

Y'all heard about the lady what lost her cat and took the cat in a little casket up to a big church, and said, "I want you to bury my cat."

They run her off, said, "We ain't near about gonna do that."

She took it to another church, and they run her off. Then she took the cat to a Baptist church out on the edge of town and told the preacher she couldn't find nobody to hold a service for a dead cat.

The man talked to her bad. "How dare you think we would bury a cat."

She said, "Well, I'm frustrated, and I am prepared to give two thousand dollars to whoever holds a service for my cat."

And the preacher said, "Lady, why didn't you tell me your cat was a Baptist?"

—*Jerry Clower*

Three Little Pigs

These three little pigs go into a restaurant. The waiter, a little nervous about serving pigs in the establishment, puts them at a corner table. The first little pig orders lasagna. The second little pig orders spaghetti. The third little pig says he just wants a big glass of water. The pigs enjoy the meal and leave.

Next day, the three little pigs show up at the same restaurant, and the waiter again gives them the corner table. He asks the first little pig what he wants for lunch, and he replies, "I'll have a hamburger and french fries." The second little pig says, "I'll have a hot dog and some Tater Tots." The third little pigs says he'll just have a big glass of water. They enjoy themselves and leave.

Next day the three little pigs show up again. The waiter thinks this is strange, but he puts them at the corner table once more. The first little pig says, "I'd like a chicken salad sandwich." The second little pig says, "I'd like a tuna salad sandwich." The third little pig says, "I just want a big glass of water."

The waiter, overcome with curiosity, says, "Look, the other two little pigs order nice meals and enjoy themselves, and all you do is drink a big glass of water. What gives?"

The third little pig responds, "Hey, someone's got to go *wee wee wee* all the way home!"

—*Billy Gilman*

The Weather Dog

Weather has gotten so dang important all of a sudden. I'm out raking leaves the other day and Bubbette comes running out of the house and yelling, "Tornado! Tornado, it's a big one!" I nearly jumped out of my skin, and began to run under the house, yelling back, "Which direction?" She said, "It's in Kansas." I could have killed her!

All you need is one of Bubba's Weather Dogs. You get a dog, and if you want to know what the weather is, you just send him outside for a while. If he comes back wet, then it's raining outside. If he comes back white, it's snowing. If he comes back with his tongue out panting for air, then it's very hot. And if he don't come back at all, then it's windy. Stay inside!

—*T. Bubba Bechtol, CSP*

The Shrewd, Stubborn, Inventive Parrot

This family was walking down the street one day, and they came to a pet shop. A parrot sat in a cage just outside the shop, and as they passed by the parrot yelled out, "Hey! Hey, you!"

The father looked around and said, "Who, me?"

"Yeah, you," the parrot said. "You're ugly. You and your whole family are ugly. Your little girl's ugly, your little boy's ugly, and your wife is *really* ugly."

The father is startled. Then he gets angry. "I can't believe this lousy bird." He walks into the shop and finds the owner. "Listen," he begins, "my family and I are walking down the sidewalk in front of your shop, and your parrot starts using foul language and putting my family down. I don't really appreciate that."

The pet owner apologizes profusely, and says, "Don't worry, I'll take care of Mr. Parrot, but good." He goes outside, grabs the parrot by the neck and jerks him out of the cage. He then proceeds to slap him against the wall, stomps him on the sidewalk, and chokes him half to death before putting him back in the cage saying, "Don't you ever talk that way to anybody again."

The owner leaves him lying on the floor of the cage and walks back inside. But as the family starts to walk away, the parrot raises up and yells, "Hey, you!"

The father stops and looks back. "Yeah, what?"

The parrot says, "You know!"

—Dickey Lee 🏵

Slower than Snail Mail

A snail knocks on this guy's door. The guy is annoyed, so he picks the snail up and throws him as far as he can. Seven years later, the snail knocks on his door again and says, "What was that all about?"

—Jack "Cowboy" Clement 🏵

The Case of the Breaking Leg

Here is a little true story I didn't include in my just-finished autobiography.

First of all, my brother Rusty is one of the funniest people I've ever met. Saying this, we had just released "Louisiana Man," in 1961. All of sudden, we were getting lots of work. We had been on a three-week run, and we were tired.

I was backstage in Houston, Texas, in my dressing room, when the promoter knocked on the door and said, "Show time!"

"Did you tell Rusty yet?" I asked.

He said, "I tried, but he wasn't in his dressing room."

He and I started looking all over the place for Rusty. Twenty minutes goes by, and we still hadn't found him. Finally, we went and checked the store room, and there lays Rusty on a table, sleeping. I said, "Rusty, we're late. It's past show time, let's go."

"I can't, I broke my leg," he said.

I said, "You broke your leg? How'd you break it?"

"I don't know," he replied sleepily. "I was just laying here and it started breaking."

After we got through laughing, we went out and did 'em a hell of a show.

—Doug Kershaw

Funny
Country Songs

*Billy Edd
Wheeler &
Chet Atkins*

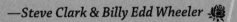

I hope you're living as high on the
hog as the pig you turned out to be!

—*Steve Clark & Billy Edd Wheeler*

Flushed from the Bathroom of Your Heart

by Jack "Cowboy" Clement 🌹

Through the back door of your life you've swept me out, dear.
In the breadline of your dreams I've lost my place.
From the table of your love I'm thrown the breadcrumbs.
At the Indianapolis of your heart I've lost the race.
In the garbage disposal of your mind I've been ground up, dear.
In the ballpark of your love I've been struck out.
Upon the river of your plans I'm up the creek now.
Now I'm corroded in the junkyard of your heart.
I've been washed down the sink of your conscience.
In the theater of your love I've lost my part.
And you say you've got me out of your system.
I've been flushed from the bathroom of your heart.

High on the Hog

by Steve Clark & Billy Edd Wheeler 🌹

Well, remember when you told me that I'd never have nothing
And how you laughed when I said nothing is enough if I've
    got you?
Then you walked right out of my life, said you couldn't stand
    the music,
And you married you that sacker down at the Convenient
    Grocery Store.

CHORUS

Well, I hope to heck you're living as high on the hog
As the pig you turned out to be.
I just wanted you to know, if you hear me on the radio-wo-wo
This song is dedicated to your ears.
How I hated your ears . . . your little piggy-wiggy ears.

So I made a million dollars with this Sears & Roebuck guitar,
And it was easy to forget you in my big ole Cadillac.
And I hope your husband's sacking has improved since I been
    back.
The last time he broke six eggs and he mashed a loaf of bread.

REPEAT CHORUS, AS ABOVE

I Still Write Your Name in the Snow

by Chet Atkins, CGP* & Billy Edd Wheeler, PGS*
(*Certified Guitar Player & Pretty Good Songwriter)

I'm almost sorry now I caught you messing 'round.
You packed up your pickup and boogied out of town.
Well, darling, I thought you'd like to know
That I still write your name in the snow.

CHORUS #1
When the snowflakes fall I always see
The happy you and me that used to be,

And when the snow has covered all the ground
I hear your name and have to write it down.
Do you think of me when you're feeling low
And wish you could write my name in the snow?

Once I had an inkling you'd come back again.
I see now that I was just tinkling in the wind.
You hurt me more than you will ever know,
But I still write your name in the snow.

Chorus #2
When the snowflakes fall I always see
The happy you and me that used to be.
I write your name so beautifully,
But it's hard to dot the i and cross the t.
Do you think of me when you're feeling low
And wish you could write my name in the snow?

Tag
Son-of-a-gun I'm tired o' living this way, hot-a-mighty damn!

Hot Dog Heart

by Billy Edd Wheeler 🌹

Went walking down the street one day, said, Hey there m'lady,
You sure look good to me and I'd like to make you my baby.

She said *Swell* and I felt good. I thought I'd hooked a keeper,
But the price o' eggs went up that day and they ain't never got
    no cheaper.

CHORUS

She was a T-bone talking woman, but she had a hot dog heart,
    heart, heart;
A T-bone talking woman, but she had a hot dog heart.

Well, diamonds look like glass, a star looks like a planet,
But you can't tell a heart of gold from one that's made of granite.
And you can't tell a queen these days from some old high-class
    floozy.
I ain't a king but I know by now, I should a-been a little
    more choosy.

CHORUS (AS ABOVE)

I'm not an educated feller, I didn't go too far in school,
But I can count and read and write, and tell a horse from a mule.
But trying to judge a woman, boys, it's bound to bring you tears.
There's many different kinds of girls, but they all got the same
    size ears!

END WITH CHORUS

Dirty Old Egg-Sucking Dog

*⟩ by Jack "Cowboy" Clement, 🌹 as recorded by
Johnny Cash on Columbia Records*

Well, he's not very handsome to look at, aw, he's shaggy and he
      eats like a hog.
And he's always killing my chickens, that dirty old egg-sucking
      dog.
If he don't stop eating my eggs up, though I'm not a real bad guy,
I'm going to get my rifle and send him to that great henhouse in
      the sky.

Egg-sucking dog, I'm gonna stomp your head in the ground
If you don't stay out of my henhouse, you dirty old egg-sucking
      hound.
Egg-sucking dog, you're always hanging around.
But you better stay out of my henhouse, you dirty old egg-
      sucking hound.

What I Look Like to You
(The Betty Crocker Song)

by Billy Edd Wheeler 🌹 & Paul Craft

One day I found my husband loafing 'round at home,
Said, "Honey, don't you think it's time you fixed that telephone?"
He got that look upon his face I've come to know so well,

He said, "Do I look like Alexander Graham Bell?"
"Well then, how 'bout that reading lamp on my side of the bed?
If it's not too much trouble, wish you'd fix it like you said."
"He gave me the same old look, and then I heard him say
Do I look like Edison . . . as in Thomas A?"

CHORUS #1
If that's who you think I look like, better check those baby blues.
I find that kind of offer easy to refuse.
I got too much talent and better things to do
Than to try to be like the me that I look like to you.

My neighbor John came over, and John's a handy man
Fixed the phone, my reading lamp, rewired my 'lectric fan
My husband said, "For all that work how much did he get paid?"
I said, "John said I could bake him a cake, or he'd take it out
　　in trade."
"What kind of cake'd you bake him?" he said smugly from
　　his rocker.
I smiled real sweet and said, "Do I look like Betty Crocker?"

CHORUS #2
If that's who you think I look like, better check those
　　bloodshot eyes.
Confucius say, Small mind in for big surprise.
I got too much talent and better things to do.
Than to try to be like the me that I look like to you.

Where's a Restrictor Plate When You Really Need One?

A request came to my ex-office to serve as Grand Marshal for the race at Richmond. Being a NASCAR fan, I, of course, agreed.

I arrived at the airport a little bit frazzled from a hectic weekend. As I waited to board the plane, eager to lean the seat back and go to sleep, that sweet person to whom we owe everything (a fan) came up to me and began a virtually uninterrupted flow of commentary.

"Oh, I just loved that show you did with James Gar(d)ner." (Sorry about the *D*, Jim, that's what she said!) "It was *Maverick*, wasn't it?"

"Actually, it was *Bret* Mav . . . "

" . . . and you did that song about mamas and babies and cowboys before Willie and Waylon did, didn't you?"

"Yaawwn."

"How'd you get Willie to give you his song, anyway?"

"Uh, that's my so . . . "

"Are you gonna do another movie with James Gardner?"

"I'd sure li . . . "

"He's cute, ain't he?"

"Wellll . . . "

"Are you going to sing here sometime? I'd sure like to see you in person."

"Huh?"

At this point, possibly confused by my fatigue-exacerbated dim-wittedness she abruptly ceased the onslaught. She cocked her head to one side and looked at me nervously. "You are Bruce Lee, aren't you?"

I karate-chopped her and got on the plane. I think it was Richmond.

—Ed Bruce

Hank Williams's Song Ideas and Sense of Humor

One time, Hank was reading *True Romance* comic books, and I said, "Hank, why are you reading all these sissy books for? My sister reads *True Romance* comic books."

He said, "Hell, boy, where do you think I get my ideas for songs from? Listen to this: *Why can't I melt your cold, cold heart?*" I thought, Hey—yeah! He told me he always carried a little bitty notebook and a little bitty sharpened pencil. He said, "I get ideas from these books here, and people's conversations. Somebody'll say something about a wife, and I'll write it down."

I learned a lot hanging around Hank. When I asked him about heart songs—that's what they called love ballads back then—he said, "Boy, you got to be in love and have your heart break in a million pieces; and then be able to tell it to somebody in a song, real simple, so when they hear it, it breaks their heart, and reminds them of a broken heart." He said, "People love sympathy, they love to be sad, so they'll rush out and buy that record so they can feel sorry for themselves." I never forgot that.

I think some of his humor rubbed off on me. Just look at "Wolverton Mountain." It's got a humorous edge to it.

That's my story. I started out with the father—the greatest—and continue with the son, also the greatest. It's country music history, and I'm honored and proud to be a part of it.

—*Merle Kilgore*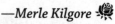

A Tribute to Chet Atkins

Chet Atkins

"Anyone who remotely knows music or the guitar understands Chet Atkins is the king of the instrument. Anyone who is lucky enough to know him personally knows he's an even greater person."

—*Steve Wariner*

"Aw, Chet, picking the guitar in front of you would be like hitting golf balls in front of Jack Nicklaus!"

—Vince Gill to Chet Atkins,
when asked to put down the
mandolin he'd just burned up,
and pick up the guitar

"Chet was always a natural leader that no one ever questioned, because we all instinctively knew he was the real thing."

—Ray Stevens 🌹

"There will never be anybody like Chet Atkins. He is not only the greatest guitar player in the world, he is also one of the greatest human beings that ever lived."

—Dolly Parton 🌹

A Touch of Spain in Tennessee

by Billy Edd Wheeler, 1977

A touch of Spain in Tennessee
Is that what you are, Mister Guitar Man?
Moving like the sleepy fog
Upcurving over Tennessee rivers
Your fingers tell the story.
Let out of leather golf glove cases
They pump and roll like exercisers' legs
Walking the air sunward.

True to the rhythm and incredibly strong,
Their light leaping swiftnesses render
Motion into cadence—melodies plucked
Out of awakened strings giving life and voice
To deep inner passions. I am transfixed, touched,
Watching winds of universal art sweep through you
As your fingers dance on to the music. Seems to me
You are the essence of taste and things musically beautiful.
A touch of Spain and a lot of Tennessee.

So Long, Chester

Billy Edd Wheeler, 2001

Your hero-friend Garrison Keillor said,
In his eloquent goodbye at the Ryman,

You said instead of going to Baptist's heaven
Where you'd tire of streets of gold and no brick houses
You might end up in Minnesota, where it's so cold
You smiled once and your upper lip didn't come back down.
Bonnie Blue Eyes said Garrison did you proud, and she
Wished, like the rest at the Ryman, he'd talked on forever.
Well, as for heaven, be it bricks or gold, my say is
Minnesota's a mite small for all the guitar players
Gone before and coming soon, who'll want to sit around
And pick with you, trying to learn your licks.
That goes for Tennessee too, where you first touched earth,
And Georgia as well, your second landing.
As Garrison said, "…May the angels bear you up,
And may eternal light shine upon you…" as you shined
On us. And—old buddy, old pal—wherever you end up,
Even if it's lip-freezing Minnesota, I'll just say this:
In my opinion, I've been a pretty good fellow.
It will be an injustice if I don't make it there too."

Dear Billy Edd,

You couldn't pick a better man than Chet Atkins to dedicate
your book to. He's one of my favorite people in the music business
—talented, unselfish, and knows songs and people. He was the first
producer to put a hold on "Green Green Grass Of Home." That
shows Chet knew something, and I sure am glad he did!

—*Curly Putman*

Dear Billy Edd,

One of my heroes is your friend, Chet Atkins. He told me once, when I was about to go on stage and was very nervous, "Bubba, aren't you a comedian?" I said I was. He said, "Don't you know your routine?" I said, "Yes, sir." He then smiled and put his hand on my arm. "Let me give you some advice, son. This entertainment thing is a fun business, and if we aren't having fun, then we aren't doing it right." It relaxed me, and I went on stage and blew them away. But I never forgot his words, and I pass them on when I can.

—*T. Bubba Bechtol, CSP*

Chet's New Bifocals

You could do a whole book on Chet's one-liners, or what I call his "zingers." This one kills me, although it's a little risqué.

I once did a show with Chet. Between numbers, he was cleaning his glasses. He told the audience, with his typical dry delivery, "I got me some new bifocals." He paused for a minute, and then said, "While I was admiring the big one, the little one peed on my shoes!"

—*Steve Wariner*

A Kiss for Vince on Leona Atkins' Seventieth

Bonnie and Joe Taggert threw a birthday party for Chet's wife, Leona, at their house in Franklin, Tennessee. While Leona was opening presents on the deck, Vince snuck into the living room and hunkered down behind a life-size cutout of himself that was standing inside a "cake."

Leona absolutely adores Vince Gill—his singing, his personality, his good looks—so when we were called to dinner, and as she passed by Vince's likeness, she reached up and planted a kiss on the lips of the cutout. Vince popped up then, startling her, and gave her a real hug and kiss. Now, Leona has never been a demonstrative person, at least not in my presence. But this time she lost it. She screamed, rolled on the floor, and came to rest pumping her legs up and down in a constant drumming.

Following dinner, we all got a present as we sat around and watched a couch-full of talented musicians jam—Chet on guitar, Vince on mandolin, Victor Krauss (Alison's brother) playing stand-up bass, and noted fingerpicker Chip Young and Pat Bergeson passing another guitar between them. (This was 1994, a few years before Pat married Alison. Pat is one of Chet's discoveries, who now plays in Lyle Lovett's band.)

When Chet invited Vince to lay down the mandolin and pick up a guitar, Vince said, "Aw, Chet, playing the guitar in front of you would be like hitting golf balls in front of Jack Nicklaus." But he did play the guitar, dazzling us all. I mean the guy can *pick!*

Bonnie said Vince told her that was a night he'll always remember. It was the first time he got to pick with his idol.

—*Ed.*

A Hot-Shot Gig from Chet Atkins

This is a true story. When I first came to Nashville I often stopped by Chet Atkins's office, hoping to learn a new tune or technique, or just to say hello to this great artist who had become so much a part of my music. Chet was generous with his time, patiently playing things slowly sometimes, so I could catch the notes as they went by. I learned a lot of music this way.

One day he said, "Muriel, I have a job for you." Wow, I thought, Carnegie Hall? The Grand Ole Opry? Austin City Limits? "My pet rooster, Hot Shot, has come down with a case of feather mites. My wife and I are too old to crawl into that little chicken coop, not to mention being too big, and you're the smallest person I know, besides Little Jimmy Dickens."

Sure enough, that afternoon they put a plastic bag over me to protect my clothes, and with a great deal of coaching I caught the rooster by both legs, to keep the spurs from getting me. I held the neck with the other hand, so Chet's wife, Leona, could spread bacon grease around its neck for the mite dust to adhere to. Then I caught the hen, also named Leona, and we covered her with mite dust as well, while Hot Shot complained loudly.

With that, Leona put a little more water in the stew, and I was invited to stay for lunch. Chicken stew, I think it was.

—Muriel Anderson

A Chet Atkins Four-Pack

In a book dedicated to Chet Atkins, and with so many references made to him by a large number of our contributors, it seems a shame to have only one joke directly from him—back at the beginning—so I have sifted through several dozen of his jokes and come up with the following four-pack. In the words of a song made famous by Jim Ed Brown: Pop-a-top, my friends, and enjoy a little more of our CGP.

No Kin, He Claimed

Monroe, a sixty-year-old man, had worked at Big Ham's car dealership in Nashville, Tennessee, for twenty-one years and never missed a day. But today he walked into Big Ham's office looking worried. Big Ham asked him what was wrong.

"Well, boss, I got a problematical situation," he said. "I got to go see the judge on account of this girl claiming I got her in a family way. She's hitting me with a paternity suit. I'm gonna need the day off."

Naturally, the boss let him go.

A few days later, Monroe came back from test-driving a car with a customer when he ran into Big Ham, who asked him, "How did your day in court go, Monroe?"

"Not good, sir. Not good."

"What happened?"

"Well sir," Monroe answered, "there she sat . . . holding that baby in her arms. And I said to the judge, I said, your honor . . . you look at that baby and you look at me. That baby don't look *nothing* like me."

"So, what did the judge say?"

"The judge said, 'You keep feeding him till he does.'"

At the Ballet

Chet took his brother-in-law Jethro Burns to a ballet, while they had some time to kill in Atlanta. Jethro had never been to a ballet and was pretty impressed.

"Well," Chet asked Jethro, "how did you like it?"

"Fine," he said. "I loved the costumes, the scenery, and the dancing, and all, but how come everybody was walking around on tippy-toes? Why don't they just get taller people?"

Not a Matter of Choice

There was an old fellow who was in such good health, his friends wanted to take him to a doctor and get him examined to find out what made him so healthy. He was seventy-five. Well, the doctor examined him and was quite impressed, and he said to the man, "What did your father die of?"

"I never said he died," the man replied.

"Well, then, what did your grandfather die of?"

The man answered, "I never said anything about him dying, either. In fact, he's getting married next week." The doctor asked how old his grandfather was. "A hundred and seventeen years old, and he's marrying a girl of twenty-three."

"Well," the doctor asked, "at his age, why does he want to marry such a young girl?"

The man replied, "I didn't say he *wanted* to!"

The Drunk Prize Winner

A drunk wandered into a bar where there was a dart-throwing contest going on. Encouraged by the bartender, he took a turn and, as luck would have it, hit the bull's eye. His prize for winning first place was a live turtle.

About a month later, this same drunk stumbled into the bar again, and it so happened that another dart-throwing contest was under way. The drunk took his turn and, miraculously, hit the bull's eye again. The bartender thought he looked familiar, so he said, "Sir, weren't you in here a while back?" The drunk nodded. "And didn't you win a prize?" He nodded again. "Well, I don't want to give you the same thing again so, tell me, what did you win before?"

The drunk scratched his head and said, "The best I can remember, it was a roast beef sandwich on a real hard bun!"

My Fifteen Seconds of Fame

When Elvis came to Asheville, North Carolina, to sing at the Civic Center, Lamar Fike invited me to come to his room at Rodeway Inn, about five miles from where I live in Swannanoa. While I was swapping jokes with Elvis's record producer, Felton Jarvis, and a couple of bodyguards, the phone rang. I picked up the receiver and, affecting the voice of an English butler, said, "Lamar Fike's residence. May I be of assistance?"

"Let me speak with Lamar," the voice requested, and I knew at once who it was. But it went on to say, "This is Elvis."

I cut the comedy routine. "Elvis, this is Billy Edd Wheeler. Lamar just stepped out. Uh, thank you for recording my songs."

"Thank you for writing them," he said politely. "Just tell Lamar to call me when he gets back."

That evening, Lamar invited me to come backstage and visit with him in Elvis's dressing room.

Then came the moment. From the first chords that introduce "It's Midnight," the song I co-wrote with Jerry Chesnut, I listened intently as Elvis spoke. "Now, here's a song written by a local boy I know you'll recognize—a good friend of mine—uh . . . (he reached into his pocket and read from a scrap of paper) . . . Billy Edd Wheeler."

I looked at Lamar.

"He does that with everybody," Lamar said. "Even people like Liza Minelli. He can't remember names."

Of course, I didn't mind. I was glad to know Elvis considered me a "good friend." Good enough, that is, to carry me around in his pocket for an evening.

—Billy Edd Wheeler

B Sides
and Album Cuts

*Dolly Parton
& Vince Gill*

“ I didn't leave country–I just took it with me. ”

—Dolly Parton, to those worried about her future path following her breakthrough hit, "Here You Come Again," in 1977

Elvis's Sense of Humor

One time, up at his house in Bel Air, we were standing around in his rec room talking, when El turned to some of his friends and said, with a mischievous smile, "Don's mad at me 'cause I put him in a higher tax bracket!"

El was really good to me and treated me with great respect and warmth. He was a skilled musician in the studio; he came prepared. I recorded with him all day (keyboards) for the soundtrack to *It Happened At The World's Fair*. He stayed cheerful and gave them one good take after another, in spite of glitches from the booth and from the musicians. We did two of my songs, among the dozen or so on the soundtrack, and he asked for my input. He treated everyone with respect and encouragement. I really miss him. It's tragic he died so young.

—*Don Robertson*

The Skinniest Girl in Town

A high roller called the bellhop to his room and said, "I'd like a woman."

The bellhop told him, "Sir, this is not that kind of hotel."

The man peeled off a hundred-dollar bill and said, "Are you sure?" The bellhop took the money and asked what kind of woman the man wanted. "She has to be at least seven-feet tall and weigh under a hundred and ten pounds."

The bellhop soon returned with a woman seven-feet-two inches tall who weighed ninety-eight pounds. She could hide behind a rope. The man said to her, "You'll do. Now, take off your clothes and get down on your hands and knees."

"Huh-uh," she said, "I'm not that kind of a girl."

The man peeled off another C-note and said, "Are you sure?" She stripped and dropped to her hands and knees. He walked around her admiringly and said, "You're perfect." Then he walked to the bathroom and opened the door. Out sprang a large collie dog, and the man said to it, "You take a good look at her, Roscoe. Now, dang it, if you don't start eating your Gravy Train that's exactly what you're gonna look like!"

—Jerry Chesnut 🌹

Shutterbug or Humanitarian?

If Saddam Hussein was drowning and you had the choice of saving him or taking his picture, what shutter speed would you use?

—Jack "Cowboy" Clement 🌹

Lost in the Alps

When the members of a Nashville travel club started planning their annual trip, they thought it would be a different and fun experience to go hiking in the Swiss Alps. So twenty or thirty of them flew to Switzerland.

The first night, after climbing all over the place, they were gathered around the campfire in a desolate, icy wasteland, when it occurred to them it would be a good idea if they paired up and formed a buddy system. That way, nobody would get lost.

They paired up and continued hiking, and each night around the fire each person checked to make sure his or her buddy was there. After about the third day, when they were getting sick of being there, a search around found that Cohen was missing.

The next day they walked all over the icy slopes calling out, "Cohen, Cohen, where are you, Cohen?" But Cohen didn't respond. So they called in Red Cross volunteers and the search continued. Another day went by. Finally, along about sundown the next day, this fellow was trudging through the ice and snow calling out, "Cohen, Cohen, where are you, Cohen? It's the Red Cross."

From a dark depression in an icy crevice came the voice, "I gave at the office."

—*Paul Craft*

(Loyal Jones of Berea, Kentucky, gives this joke an Appalachian setting when he tells it like this: A gigantic snow storm hit Eastern Kentucky, and this particular hollow was so buried under snow, all you could see were a few chimneys. Roads were impassable. The Red Cross had to helicopter in to reach one remote cabin, and even then had to dig a tunnel through the snow to get to the house. When they knocked and cried out,

"Red Cross, Red Cross!" the lady of the house opened the door and said, "I'm sorry, I don't believe we'll be able to help you people out again this year!" —Ed.)

Reading the Strange Stone

An English guy visiting America happened by a cemetery and saw several people looking curiously at a tombstone. He ambled over and saw written on the stone the words, "Here lies Strange," obviously the name of the man buried there.

One of the Americans looked at the others and said, "Well, isn't that strange?" And they all laughed. But the Englishman stood scratching his head, unable to figure it out.

When he got back to England he said to a friend, "I don't get it. I went by this cemetery in America, and these Yanks were looking at this tombstone that said, 'Here lies Strange.' Then they laughed and said, 'Well, isn't that extraordinary.'"

—Randy Goodrum 🌹

The Game Warden Gave Up

A woman went along with her husband who was fishing on the lake. She read her book while he fished. At noon, he decided to go ashore for a snack, so she decided to row out by herself a little ways and enjoy the sunshine until he signaled for her to come back and pick him up.

To her surprise, as she sat in the boat, a game warden pulled up and asked to see her fishing license. She told him she didn't have a license. "Then I'll have to give you a citation," he said, and pulled out his ticket book.

"Wait," she said, "you can't give me a citation. I'm not fishing."

"But you have the equipment," he replied, and prepared to write her up.

"If you insist on giving me a ticket for fishing," she protested, "I'll yell *Rape!*"

"That's ridiculous," the game warden said. "I haven't even touched you or made any attempt to rape you."

"But you have the equipment," she said.

He nodded, smiled, and chugged away.

—*Bob Jennings*

Talk About Being Mad

A man got on the train in Chicago and looked up the head porter. He handed him a fifty-dollar bill and said, "Now, I'm going to my berth to get some sleep, but I want you to make sure you get me up so I can get off the train in Cincinnati. Got that?"

The porter nodded, so the man went on to say, "I'm a very sound sleeper, and I'm hard to wake up in the morning, but I'm giving you this money to make sure you get me up. Tomorrow, I'm marrying the boss's daughter in Cincinnati. It's the most important day of my life, and I have to be there."

So he went to bed, and when he woke up, he was in Louisville. Was he ever mad! He went looking for the porter, cussed him up one side and down the other, and said, "This is the maddest I've ever been. I'm so mad I could kill you."

The porter said, "Huh, you think you're mad. You should have seen the fellow I put off the train in Cincinnati!"

—*Tom T. Hall*

To Whom Are You Speaking?

A lady walked into a bar with a duck under her arm. As she passed one of the patrons, she heard him say, "Hey, where'd you get that pig?"

She turned around and said, "I beg your pardon, this is not a pig, it's a duck."

The man said, "I was talking to the duck."

—*Tom T. Hall* 🌹

Big Apple Bagel Lady

A little old lady sits on the sidewalk in New York City, selling bagels for twenty-five cents apiece. Through all kinds of weather, day in and day out, she sits there. This particular guy comes by every day and drops a quarter in her basket, but never takes a bagel.

This goes on every day for about a year. He drops a quarter and just walks away.

One day he comes by, drops a quarter, and starts to walk away. The lady says, "Pardon me, sir, could I speak to you for just a moment?"

He says, "I wondered how long it would take for you to speak to me. You're going to ask me why I always walk by, drop a quarter, and never take a bagel. Isn't that right?"

"No, sir," she says. "I just want to remind you that, starting next Monday, bagels are thirty-five cents!"

—*Larry Henley*

Nothing to Brag About

Charlie Dick contributed the following joke, saying it was Patsy's favorite. —Ed.

A traveling salesman stopped at this house and knocked on the door. When the twelve-year-old boy opened it and stepped out, the salesman said, "Hey, kid, is your mother at home?"

The boy said, "No, sir, she's over next door at the whorehouse."

The salesman thought he must have heard the kid wrong. Or thought maybe he was kidding. But he was looking the boy right in the eye, and he wasn't smiling, so he said, "Did you say whorehouse?"

"Yes, sir," the boy replied. "That's what I said."

"Well, is she a prostitute?" the man asked.

"No, she's a substitute."

The salesman shook his head and said, "Well, I'm a son-of-a-bitch."

"I am too," the little boy replied, "but I don't go 'round knocking on people's doors bragging about it!"

—Patsy Cline

ABOUT THE CONTRIBUTORS

BILL ANDERSON 🌹

Known as "Whispering Bill" because of his breathy voice and soft singing style, Bill Anderson's credentials shout his prominence as one of the most awarded songwriters in country music for songs like "City Lights," "The Tips of My Fingers," and the classic, "Still." A popular TV host, recording artist and entertainer, Bill authored the book *I Hope You're Living as High on the Hog as the Pig You Turned Out to Be*, which takes a humorous look at the music business. The title was taken from the song listed in the "Funny Country Songs" section. Bill was inducted into the Country Music Hall of Fame in 2001.

MURIEL ANDERSON

Raised in a musical family in Downers Grove, Illinois, Muriel is widely respected as the premier woman fingerstyle guitarist on the scene today. She has released seven CDs in the US, three in Japan, and an ever-increasing number of books and videos. She is host and originator of the renowned Muriel Anderson's All Star Guitar Night and founded the Music For Life Alliance charity. Her *Heartstrings* album accompanied the astronauts on a space shuttle mission. She won the National Guitar Picking Championship, the first nylon-string guitarist and first female to win.

EDDY ARNOLD

Few artists have attained Eddy Arnold's stature or can boast of *Seven Decades of Hits*, the title of his latest album, in which he revisits songs like "Anytime," "In the Misty Moonlight," "Make the World Go Away," "Bouquet of Roses," and "What's He Doing in My World." "Songs," the mild-mannered Eddy says, "with which I have had a great relationship." The album also features a duet of "Cattle Call" with LeAnn Rimes, illustrating that Eddy's talent is as mellow and mature as yesterday, yet sweet and fresh as today. One of country's classiest acts.

CHET ATKINS

Known as "Mr. Guitar," Chet Atkins was the most-recorded guitarist in history with one hundred albums to his credit–and also a master joke teller. Also known as "The Country Gentleman," this soft-spoken legend has a street named after him and a statue erected in his honor in Nashville. He's in the Country Music Hall of Fame and received a Lifetime Achievement Award from the National Academy of Recording Arts and Sciences. According to editor John Schroeter, *Fingerstyle Guitar Magazine* has named Chet Atkins "Guitarist of the Millennium."

DAVID BALL

Singer-songwriter David Ball was born in 1959, in Rock Hill, South Carolina. When he was in the seventh grade he wrote his first song and played it in a school talent show with his own band, The Strangers. After a stint in the '70s in Uncle Walt's Band in Austin, Texas, he moved on to Nashville and recorded three singles in the late '80s as a solo act for RCA Records. His first hit came when he recorded his "Thinkin' Problem" for Warner Bros. Records, followed by "Look What Followed Me Home." After that came "Starlite Lounge," which was also well received. He is currently recording a new CD, produced by his friend Wood Newton.

T. BUBBA BECHTOL, CSP

"Bubba's going to be the next Foxworthy," Bubba's manager Tandy Rice declares. Tandy managed Jerry Clower for twenty-five years, so he knows funny when he sees it. Bubba has done over ninety national TV appearances and has entertained in the White House for Presidents Carter, Reagan, and Bush Sr. President Reagan honored him with the Citizen's Medal for his "Contribution to the American Way of Life." Among many other awards, he received the Certified Speaking Professional designation from the National Speakers Association in 1985.

BOBBY BRADDOCK

From the 1960s through the '80s, Bobby was a recording artist for MGM, Columbia, Mercury, Elektra, and RCA. He played in several rock 'n' roll bands in his native Florida before moving to Nashville in 1964, where he played piano for Marty Robbins for two years. He had chart success and hits with Robbins, the Oak Ridge Boys, Willie Nelson, Tanya Tucker, Jerry Lee Lewis, and others. He teamed with Curly Putman to write a #1 hit for Tammy Wynette, "D-I-V-O-R-C-E." He and Curly also wrote the song that restored George Jones's flagging career, "He Stopped Loving Her Today," which won CMA's Song of the Year two years in a row.

ED BRUCE

Actor and singer-songwriter William Edwin Bruce was born December 29, 1939, in Keiser, Arkansas. He spent several years promoting tourism as "The Tennessean." His first recordings were on Sun Records, but his first commercial success came when he wrote "Save Your Kisses" for Tommy Roe, and the hit "See the Big Man Cry," for Charlie Louvin. His own stardom came with "The Last Cowboy Song," and "You're the Best Break This Old Heart Ever Had." His song "Mamas, Don't Let Your Babies Grow Up To Be Cowboys," recorded by Waylon Jennings and Willie Nelson, became the anthem of outlaw country. Ed starred with James Garner in the TV series *Maverick* and recorded "Theme from Bret Maverick."

BRUCE BURCH

Bruce has experienced success in almost every facet of the music business. He authored a book, *Songs that Changed Our Lives*, excerpts of which have appeared in the popular Chicken Soup for the Soul series. He ran his own music publishing company before landing his current job as Creative Director for EMI Music, presently the owner of the world's largest publishing catalog. In this capacity, he represents some of the world's most renowned songwriters. As a songwriter, he has had songs recorded by Faith Hill, Aaron Tippin, Collin Ray, Barbara Mandrell, and Reba McEntire, who took his "Rumor Has It," and "It's Your Call" to #1.

ARCHIE CAMPBELL

A star and chief writer for *Hee Haw* beginning in 1968, Archie Campbell was born in 1914 in Bull's Gap, Tennessee, and died in 1987. After having radio shows in Knoxville and Chattanooga, he signed a recording contract with RCA Victor in 1959, just after his Grand Ole Opry debut. His chart activity included "Trouble In The Amen Corner," "The Men In My Little Girl's Life," and a comedy album with Junior Samples, *Bull Session at Bull's Creek*. (I played dozens of rounds of golf with Archie, and the jokes always flew.—Ed.)

JERRY CHESNUT 🌹

Natural country wit and raconteur, NSAI Hall of Famer Jerry Chesnut was born May 3, 1931, in Loyall, Kentucky. After graduating from high school at Loyall High in 1949, he worked as a railroad conductor and vacuum cleaner distributor. He moved to Nashville in 1958 and had his first hit in 1967, "A Dime At A Time," recorded by Del Reeves. His first #1 came in 1968, "Another Place Another Time," by Jerry Lee Lewis. Other notable songs include: "It's Midnight," co-written with Billy Edd Wheeler and recorded by Elvis Presley; "A Good Year For The Roses," recorded by George Jones, Elvis Costello, and Alan Jackson; "It's Four In The Morning," Faron Young and Tom Jones; "Holding On To Nothing," Dolly Parton and Porter Wagoner; and "T-R-O-U-B-L-E," cut by Elvis Presley in 1975 and Travis Tritt in 1993.

GUY CLARK

Guy Clark wrote the classic "Desperados Waiting For A Train," "LA Freeway," and the brilliant train song, "Texas 1947," all on his first album, *Old No. 1*, released in 1975 and still cited by critics and performers as a landmark work. He also wrote "Heartbroke," "Homegrown Tomatoes," and more, and has a huge fan club as a performer and recording artist.

JACK "COWBOY" CLEMENT 🌹

One of the legends of Music City, Jack has written hit songs, produced movies, produced new talent like the great Charley Pride, performed on stage and TV, and owns Clementvision, a recording studio where artists from all over come to record. Among his big songs are "I Know One," recorded by Jim Reeves and Garth Brooks, "Just Between You and Me," and novelty songs like "Dirty Old Egg-Sucking Dog," and "Flushed from The Bathroom of Your Heart."

PATSY CLINE

Born Virginia Patterson Hensley on September 8, 1932, near Winchester, Virginia, Patsy auditioned successfully for Opry manager Jim Denny at age sixteen, but couldn't afford to stay in town long enough to make an appearance. After marrying Gerald Cline in 1953, she signed a recording contract with 4-Star and had several releases that failed. Charlie Dick became her second husband in 1957, the year she appeared on the *Arthur Godfrey Talent Scouts* show, singing "Walking After Midnight," released by Decca to become a #2 country, #12 pop hit. In the fall of 1960, she recorded "I Fall To Pieces," her first #1. Her short and stormy but successful career ended when the small aircraft piloted by her manager, Randy Hughes, crashed in the woods near Camden, Tennessee, on March 5, 1963. Hughes's father-in-law, Cowboy Copas, and Hawkshaw Hawkins also died with Patsy in the crash. Patsy's versions of "Walking After Midnight," "I Fall To Pieces," "Crazy," "She's Got You," and "Sweet Dreams," are considered five of the greatest recordings ever made in country music. Her *Greatest Hits* album stayed at #1 on *Billboard* for more than four years, actually remaining on the charts for thirteen years.

JERRY CLOWER

The late Jerry Clower, from Yazoo City, Mississippi, graduated from Mississippi State with a degree in agriculture. After selling fertilizer to farmers for eighteen years, he produced his first album, *Jerry Clower from Yazoo City, Mississippi: Talkin'*. A second album led to a contract with MCA Records, where he had twelve chart-busting LPs. He was named Country Comic of the Year nine years in succession. He wrote four books, co-hosted TV's *Nashville On The Road*, and in the spring of 1998 was voted #1 Living Country Comedian by *Music City News*. He passed away in Jackson, Mississippi, in August 1998.

PAUL CRAFT

Chet Atkins said, "I've known Paul for several years. He has continually amazed me with his writing ability, and he is a super entertainer." Born in Memphis, Paul dropped out of the University of Virginia to tour with Jimmy Martin, playing banjo; he then came back and graduated. In 1966, he wrote what he considered his first good song, "Raised By the Railroad Line," recorded by the bluegrass group, The Seldom Scene. In 1977, Chet Atkins signed him to RCA Records. That same year, he had two Grammy nominations: "Hank Williams You Wrote My Life" and "Dropkick Me, Jesus." He also wrote "Midnight Flyer" for the Eagles and "Keep Me From Blowing Away" for Linda Ronstadt. In 1990 he had a #1 hit with Mark Chestnut, "Brother Jukebox."

FLOYD CRAMER

Born in Huttig, Arkansas, Floyd played on the *Louisiana Hayride* with Jim Reeves before coming to Nashville in 1955, where he helped Chet Atkins and Owen Bradley create the "Nashville Sound." Famous for a "slip note" style of piano playing, invented by Don Robertson, Floyd played on sessions for Elvis, Roy Orbison, Patsy Cline, Perry Como, and too many others to list. He recorded over fifty albums and was most famous for the song he wrote, "Last Date." He died of cancer in 1997, at the age of sixty-four. Soft spoken and shy-appearing, he loved golf and the joke-telling that goes with it in Nashville.

MAC DAVIS

Mac was born and raised in Lubbock, Texas. In the 1960s, he wrote three hits for Elvis Presley: "In The Ghetto," "Memories," and "Don't Cry Daddy." Other hits followed: "Watching Scotty Grow" and Ray Price's "The Lonesomest Lonesome" in 1972. That same year, Mac's recording career took off with his "Baby Don't Get Hooked On Me." By 1981, he had a hit with "Hooked On Music." In 1982, he had a successful TV show, *The Mac Davis Show*, and won the Entertainer of the Year Award from the Academy of Country Music. He entered NSAI's Hall of Fame in 2000.

JIMMY DEAN

Jimmy's entertainment career began in the Air Force. He had his first hit in 1953 with "Bumming Around." In 1957-58 he starred in *The Jimmy Dean Show* on CBS, and in '61 wrote and recorded "Big Bad John," a #1 country and pop hit. Other hits were "PT 109," "The First Thing Every Morning," and "A Thing Called Love." In the '70s he started his sausage business, and by the '80s it was said that he preferred a string of sausages to a string of hits. His easy-going style and mellow voice helped bridge the gap between pop and country music.

RALPH EMERY

Born in McEwen, Tennessee, in 1933, Ralph hosted the legendary all-night WSM radio show for over fifteen years, making it the most popular country radio show in America. He recorded for Liberty in the early '60s, hitting #4 on the country charts with "Hello Fool." From 1982 to 1993 he hosted the TNN series *Nashville Now*, during which time he recorded several children's albums with the puppet Shotgun Red. He has published three best-selling books, the most recent being *Fifty Years Down A Country Road*.

JUNI FISHER

Juni Fisher was farm-raised in central California, forty-five miles north of Bakersfield. From her first stage solo at five, through a bluegrass band she led at seventeen, to singing for a big band orchestra at eighteen —and everything in between—she's been an entertainer who can hold her own. Her CD, *Tumbleweed Letters*, released in 1999, has earned her a regular spot on WSM's *Opry Star Spotlight*, a nighttime radio show hosted by Matthew Gilliam. She recently appeared on the Ryman stage as part of the Grand Ole Opry's Seventy-fifth Anniversary Show, broadcast live on WSM. Get the album at The-Record-Store/junifisher.com.

VINCE GILL

When Vince was asked what he'd like to see while hosting CBS' *CMA Awards* show in October 2000, he said, "I want to hear Chet Atkins play again." (Chet is one of Vince's heroes.) Vince hosted, his record-setting ninth consecutive time, and the show has been good to him. He has won eighteen CMA Awards himself—more than any other artist. For five years in a row (1991-95), he won the CMA Male Vocalist Award, unequaled in the history of the CMA Awards. But his personal favorite is the Song of the Year category. "It feels the most timeless," he said. "The songs are the most poignant." In '91, '92, '93, and '96, he took home Song of the Year honors for the hits "When I Call Your Name," "Look At Us," "I Still Believe In You," and "Go Rest High On That Mountain." In '93 and '94 he won the Entertainer of the Year award.

BILLY GILMAN

When preternaturally poised Billy Gilman's first release, "One Voice," debuted on *Billboard*'s Country Singles chart in May 1999, he became the youngest charting country artist ever, breaking a 43-year-old record held by Hall of Famer Brenda Lee. He was eleven. "The only thing I can compare it with is Brenda, Tanya Tucker, or LeAnn Rimes," says his manager, Scott Siman. "I joke and say it's kind of more like Forrest Gump to me, the things that kid says and does." His mother, Fran Gilman, says Billy could learn lyrics at three and at five was singing Pam Tillis songs. This rare ability is what attracted Siman to him when he was introduced by Asleep at the Wheel's Ray Benson. Billy was performing with the Wheel at Nashville's Wild Horse Saloon. Since then, he has been on *The Tonight Show*, NBC's *Today* show, *The Rosie O'Donnell Show*, and CMA's *Fan Fair*. Illustrating Billy's sense of humor, Siman wrote in July 2001: "The other night at a show, Billy was introducing his hit, "One Voice." He said, 'I'm going to do this next song—you might have heard of it—it starts with an O.' The crowd lost it." Scott also informed me that the album, *One Voice*, was approaching double platinum.

NORMAN GIMBEL

Norman Gimbel never met a stranger. This gregarious super lyricist introduced himself to me in a New York agent's office, and then helped launch my songwriting career. He gave me the title "Blue Roses," which I wrote for Hank Snow. But look at *his* titles: "Killing Me Softly With His Song," Grammy Award winner; an Academy Award for "It Goes Like It Goes," from the film *Norma Rae*; "The Girl From Ipanema," Grammy Award winner, as well as Record of the Year.

RANDY GOODRUM

Randy is a Hot Springs, Arkansas, native who began playing piano professionally at age sixteen. After college and serving in the U.S. Army Band, he moved to Nashville in 1973, and gives Chet Atkins a lot of credit for help, influence, and inspiration in his very successful career. He earned Song of the Year in 1978 from NSAI and ACM for Anne Murray's hit, "You Needed Me," and was ASCAP's Country Songwriter Of The Year in 1981 and 1987. He's had songs in movies and on CBS's *Snowden On Ice* special. His songs include: "Bluer Than Blue," "It's Sad To Belong," "Oh Sherrie," "I'll Be Over You," and "What're We Doing In Love."

TOM T. HALL

Known as "The Storyteller," because he's the best country storytelling songwriter that ever was, Tom started playing guitar in 1946 at the age of ten, influenced by a musician who died of TB in his hometown of Olive Hill, Kentucky. Hence his classic song, "The Day That Clayton Delaney Died." After stints in radio, the Army, and more radio, Tom was asked by Margie Singleton to write her a song like "Ode To Billie Joe." He wrote the great impact song, "Harper Valley PTA," but Jeannie C. Riley ended up having the big hit with it, because Margie was out of town. Tom's other great songs include: "Ballad Of Forty Dollars," "A Week In A County Jail," "I Love," and the classic "Old Dogs, Children And Watermelon Wine."

LARRY HENLEY

Larry is a Texas native whose singing career took off in the mid-'60s with the Nashville pop group The Newbeats. When the group disbanded, he turned to songwriting. His credits include the #1 songs "Till I Get It Right," "He's A Heartache (Looking For A Place To Happen)," "Is It Still Over," and the monster smash, "The Wind Beneath My Wings." Gary Morris's version of "Wings" went to #4 in 1983, winning Larry Song of the Year honors from both the CMA and the ACM. Bette Midler's version went to #1 in 1989, winning him a Grammy Award for Best Song. He was NSAI'S Songwriter of the Year in 1983.

WAYLAND HOLYFIELD

The first and only Nashville songwriter elected to ASCAP's Board of Directors, Wayland says, "I am proudest of the song 'Could I Have This Dance.' It's used in so many weddings. Touching people's lives is what songwriting is all about." An Arkansas native, he moved to Nashville in 1972, and had his first hit, "Red Necks, White Socks And Blue Ribbon Beer," in 1973. In 1975, "You're My Best Friend" became his first solely written #1. A few of his other recorded songs are: "Some Broken Hearts Never Mend," "Till The Rivers Run Dry," "You're The Best Break This Old Heart Ever Had," plus a gazillion others.

GERRY HOUSE

As a writer, Gerry has had some forty songs cut, including four millionaire performance titles, "Little Rock" by Reba McEntire, "The Big One" by George Strait, "The River And The Highway" by Pam Tillis, and "On The Side Of The Angels," by LeAnn Rimes. He's won *Billboard*'s Personality of the Year twelve times, R&R five times, the CMA Personality of the Year, and the Marconi Award for Radio Personality of the Year In America. He plays golf too!

JANIS IAN

Janis Ian was one of Chet Atkins's favorite guitarists—quite a compliment coming from the world's greatest. More importantly, she's one of his favorite people. As for me, she's the best solo artist I've ever seen perform. When I asked her for a bio, she wrote, "Janis Ian published her first song nationally at twelve, cut her first self-penned record at fourteen, and had her first number one record at fifteen. Since then she's received nine Grammy nominations, published one book, and recorded seventeen albums. She doesn't know why." Janis lives in Nashville.

BOB JENNINGS

It is impossible to overestimate the importance of the song plugger in the music business, and the late Bob Jennings was one of the great ones. He loved country music, the singers and the songs, and worked at getting them together in the perfect marriage. After working several years for 4-Star Music, Bob was hired by Wesley Rose at Acuff-Rose Music. Bob loved golf almost as much as he loved music and Chet Atkins; it was always a treat to play with him, he was so full of colorful country sayings, stories, and anecdotes. His repertoire of jokes was inexhaustible.

GRANDPA JONES

Louis Marshall Jones became "everybody's grandpa" in 1935 at the age of twenty-two, while working with fellow native Kentuckian Bradley Kincaid on the radio in Boston. In Cincinnati in 1942, he began his commercial recording career and met the love of his life, young fiddler and mandolin player Ramona Riggins. He joined the Grand Ole Opry in 1947, became a key member of TV's *Hee Haw* in 1968, and in 1978 was inducted into CMA's Hall of Fame. Among his most notable songs were "Eight More Miles To Louisville," "Mountain Dew," "Old Rattler," and "T For Texas." One of country music's most beloved figures, he died in 1998.

DOUG KERSHAW

Known as the "Ragin' Cajun," Doug is considered by many to be the king of the fiddle players. He was born in Tiel Ridge, Cameron Parish, Louisiana, an island just off the Gulf of Mexico, on January 24, 1936, the second of four sons. In the '60s, Doug made his first network appearance on the premiere of *The Johnny Cash Show*. This led to a long-term recording contract with Warner Bros. Records. Songs such as "Diggy Diggy Lo," "Cajun Joe," and "Rita Put Your Black Shoes On," are familiar to Kershaw fans. But none reached the fame of his 1961 recording of "Louisiana Man," which immortalized his family and sold millions over the years.

MERLE KILGORE

Merle began his career in Shreveport, Louisiana, at the age of fourteen, carrying Hank Williams's guitar. At age eighteen, he wrote his first #1 hit, "More And More," a million seller for Webb Pierce, in 1954. Soon thereafter, he joined the *Louisiana Hayride*. Merle wrote "Wolverton Mountain," Claude King's ten million-selling hit, and co-wrote "Ring Of Fire" with June Carter Cash. As an actor, he has been featured in the movies *Coal Miner's Daughter, Nashville, W.W. and the Dixie Dance Kings*, and others. His biggest role was playing himself in NBC-Telecom's *Living Proof*, the life story of Hank Williams Jr. A business leader for decades, he has served as Hank Jr.'s personal manager for the last fifteen years.

THE KINGSTON TRIO

Since their first hit, "Tom Dooley," a #1 best seller on Capitol Records and voted a Grammy Award by NARAS as Country Song of the Year, Nick, Bob, and Dave became the darlings of American popular music, captivating millions of fans worldwide with their harmony and wit. The Trio wasn't just a successful musical group, it was a cultural phenomenon, the boys next door who taught us how to sing, play guitar, and be cool. Dave Guard left and was replaced by John Stewart, who was replaced eventually by George Grove, but Bob Shane remains as the core of the Trio. The music, too, is still the best American folk music that ever was.

RED LANE

"A songwriter's office is in his head," Red says, so maybe that's why he likes to jump out of planes—he loves the wide-open sky. It figures, then, he'd write a song like "The Day I Jumped From Uncle Harvey's Plane," and get it recorded by Roger Miller. A Louisiana native, he played guitar in Merle Haggard's band. The Hag has recorded twenty-five of Red's songs, including their co-written "My Own Kind of Hat." He also penned "Miss Emily's Picture" for John Conlee and "New Looks For an Old Lover," for B.J. Thomas, a BMI Million Performance Song.

DICKEY LEE

Born in Memphis in 1941, Dickey Lee started out in country but switched to pop music where he had his first hit, "Patches," a million seller in 1962. Another hit, "I Saw Linda Yesterday," followed that put him on the rock 'n' roll circuit. In 1965, he had two more pop hits, "Laurie" and "The Girl From Beyond Peyton Place." But his real love was country music. His second single for RCA was the top ten "Never Ending Song of Love." Other hits followed, the most successful of which was the #1 "Rocky." But his most famous song as a writer was the classic, "She Thinks I Still Care," recorded first by George Jones.

RICHARD LEIGH

Richard Leigh won a Grammy and CMA's Song of the Year award for "Don't It Make My Brown Eyes Blue." He has won numerous other awards for songs like "I'll Get Over You" and "Somewhere in My Broken Heart," and recently had a top ten hit with the Dixie Chicks' recording of "Cold Day in July."

GEORGE LINDSEY

George grew up in the little town of Jasper, Alabama, and after grad-uating from the University of North Alabama and doing a stint in the Air Force, he went to New York to study acting with Helen Hayes at the American Theater Wing. Off-Broadway shows led to roles on TV's *The*

Rifleman, Twilight Zone, and *The Alfred Hitchcock Hour.* But his most famous role was playing "Goober" in *The Andy Griffith Show, Mayberry R.F.D.*, and *Hee Haw.* In 1998 he helped establish the George Lindsey/ University of North Alabama Television and Film Festival.

JOHN D. LOUDERMILK 🌹

"Although his music isn't exactly weird," wrote musicologist Richie Unterberger, "John D. Loudermilk is one of the weirdest figures in music. He can range from mindless, sappy pop songs to 'Tobacco Road,' a hard-bitten tune with as much authentic grit as a Mississippi Delta blues classic. That one song is worthy of a footnote in any history of popular music." John also wrote: "Waterloo," "Norman," "Then You Can Tell Me Goodbye," "Talk Back Trembling Lips," "Indian Reservation," "Break My Mind," an instrumental for Chet Atkins called "Windy And Warm," and a whole lot more. He now spends most of his time studying ethnomusicology.

ROGER MILLER 🌹

Best known for humorous novelty songs, which overshadowed his overall great songwriting talents, Roger wrote hits for others in the 1950s, then racked up a number of hits in the '60s including "Dang Me," "Chug-A-Lug" and "Do Wacka-Do." He began 1965 with his best-known song, "King of the Road," and in 1966 had "Husbands And Wives." In the mid-'80s Roger wrote music and lyrics for *Big River*, the Broadway adaptation of Mark Twain's *Huckleberry Finn* that won seven Tony Awards. He died in 1992 of throat cancer.

BILL MONROE

The "Father of Bluegrass Music," Bill was born into a musical family in Kentucky in 1911. In 1932, he teamed with two of his two brothers and toured with a show organized by WLS Chicago, of *National Barn Dance* fame. After he formed the first band he would call the Blue Grass Boys, he appeared on the Grand Ole Opry in 1939, after which George D. Hay told him, "Bill, if you ever leave the Opry, it'll be because you fire yourself." Over fifty years later, he was still there. Famous for many songs, especially "The Kentucky Waltz," "Footprints In The Snow," and "Blue Moon of Kentucky," Bill kept up a hectic schedule, in spite of having cancer in 1981 and a double coronary bypass in 1991. He died in 1996, a few days shy of his eighty-fifth birthday.

MICKEY NEWBURY

A songwriter's songwriter, Mickey was born in Houston, Texas. In 1964 he was signed to Acuff-Rose Music in Nashville and started writing in earnest. His early songs include: "Here Comes The Rain, Baby," "Funny Familiar Forgotten Feelings," "How I Love Them Old Songs," and "Sweet Memories." In 1968, Kenny Rogers and the First Edition had a hit with his "Just Dropped In (To See What Condition My Condition Was In)." His 1996 album, *Lulled By The Moonlight*, was dedicated to our first American pop songwriter, Stephen Foster. Check his works out on www.mickeynewbury.com.

WOOD NEWTON

Studio owner, producer, recording artist, and hit songwriter, Wood came from Arkansas to Nashville in 1976. Soon thereafter, he co-wrote the #1 country hit "Bobby Sue" for the Oak Ridge Boys and "Twenty Years Ago" for Kenny Rogers. Both songs received awards from BMI for a million performances. More recently, he got the same award for "What I Didn't Do," a hit for Steve Wariner. Other artists who have recorded his songs include B. J. Thomas, Charley Pride, Alabama, Ann Murray, Willie Nelson, Tanya Tucker, Rita Coolidge, and Tracy Byrd.

DOLLY PARTON

Dolly has contributed countless treasures to the world of music entertainment, with songs such as "Jolene," "Coat of Many Colors," and "I Will Always Love You." Her acting performances include her debut in *9 To 5*, as well as roles in *The Best Little Whorehouse in Texas* and *Steel*

Magnolias, with Julia Roberts, Sally Field, and Shirley MacLaine. "Shirley MacLaine says we all got along so well in *Steel Magnolias* because we were all the same person in another life," Dolly remembers. "I told Shirley I don't believe in reincarnation—and I didn't believe in it when I lived before, either!" In 1994, the TNN/Music City News Awards gave her their Living Legend Award and the Minnie Pearl Award. The British CMA awarded Dolly their Country Legend Award in 1997. She is a four-time Grammy Award winner, has earned eight CMA Awards. The list goes on and on. Recently, when TV's Regis Philbin asked about her dimensions, she said she didn't know precisely. He said, "Why don't we measure you?" "Fine," Dolly said, not missing a beat, "I'll measure you, then you can measure me!" Pure Dolly humor.

MINNIE PEARL

Sarah Ophelia Colley was born in 1912 and died in 1996. She became one of the Opry's most popular stars, dressed in her cheap cotton dress and wide-brimmed hat with the price tag still attached. She entered the CMA Hall of Fame in 1975, received the National Medal of Arts in 1992, and in 1994 was inducted into the National Comedy Hall of Fame. (I met her at Chet Atkins's Country Gentleman Tournament at Callaway Gardens and was enchanted by her comedy routines and the loving way she described her utopian community of Grinder's Switch. —Ed.)

ELVIS PRESLEY

Elvis Aron Presley was born on January 8, 1935, in Tupelo, Mississippi, and died on August 16, 1977, in Memphis, Tennessee. He was the most celebrated popular music phenomenon of his era and, for many, remains the purest embodiment of rock 'n' roll of all time. After his manager Colonel Tom Parker, a former fairground huckster, secured his release from Sun Records, Chet Atkins went into RCA Records' studio with him on January 10, 1956, to record the epochal "Heartbreak Hotel," one of the most striking pop records ever released. It went to #1 for an astonishing eight weeks. This assured Elvis a place in pop history for one of the greatest debut records ever released. Elvis's musical influences, the highs and lows of his career, have been analyzed and documented over and over by musicologists and historians. The material included in this book are tidbits and anecdotes by the editor and a few people who knew Elvis personally.

CHARLEY PRIDE

One of country music's premier artists, Charley's golden baritone has transcended race and spanned generations. Discovered and first produced by Jack Clement, Charley was signed by Chet Atkins to RCA Records where he had thirty-six #1 records and is second in sales only to Elvis Presley. He was CMA's Entertainer of the Year in 1971, Top Male Vocalist in 1971 and 1972, and in 2000 entered their Hall of Fame for songs like "Kiss an Angel Good Morning," "Is Anybody Going to San Antone," and "All I Have to Offer You Is Me." He met the love of his life, Rozine, while playing baseball in Memphis, and they've just celebrated their forty-third wedding anniversary.

CURLY PUTMAN

Curly Putman is one of the finest songwriters in country music history. "Green Green Grass of Home," was recorded by Johnny Darrell in 1966, and was covered by Porter Wagoner, Jerry Lee Lewis, and Tom Jones. Since then, it has been recorded six hundred times, in every major language in the world. Curly also wrote, with Billy Sherrill, "My Elusive Dreams," and, with Bobby Braddock, "D-I-V-O-R-C-E," and "He Stopped Loving Her Today," CMA's Song of the Year two years in a row, 1980 and '81.

JERRY REED

Jerry is a Georgia native and a multiple Grammy-winner who made a name for himself in the 1960s as a Nashville session guitarist and as a songwriter, with compositions such as "Guitar Man" for Elvis Presley and "Crazy Legs" for Gene Vincent. By the end of the decade, Jerry was both a recording artist for RCA and a songwriter with six BMI awards to his credit, four country and two pop. By the early '70s, Jerry hit it big as an artist with two of his own compositions, "Amos Moses," and "When You're Hot, You're Hot." By the mid-'70s, Jerry found yet another career—writing songs for and acting in films: *W.W. and the Dixie Dance Kings, Gator*, and *Smokey and the Bandit*. He wrote "East Bound and Down" the theme song for *Smokey and the Bandit* and starred in the film with Burt Reynolds and Jackie Gleason. He also starred in other movies, including *Bat 55*, in which he played opposite Gene Hackman.

JIM REEVES

Jim was born in 1923 in Galloway, Texas. After overcoming a problem with stammering at the University of Texas, he worked as a singing DJ for several years. In 1952, he hosted the *Louisiana Hayride* in Shreveport and joined the Grand Ole Opry in 1955. With his recording of "Four Walls," a smash in 1957, he created his warm ballad style. Hits like "He'll Have To Go" and "I Love You Because" followed. After his death in a plane crash in 1964, his "Distant Drums" was #1 in the UK. He was loved in South Africa, where he recorded in Afrikaans.

DON ROBERTSON

Composer, lyricist, recording artist, keyboardist, arranger, conductor, singer, and occasional whistler, Don was born in Peking, China. He is the writer of 134 songs recorded commercially by over 200 artists, featured on 565 singles, in over 900 albums. Songs include "I Really Don't Want To Know," "Please Help Me I'm Falling," "Does My Ring Hurt Your Finger," and many other hits. Elvis alone recorded fourteen of his songs. In addition to many honors, Don invented the slip-note style of playing the piano, made famous by Floyd Cramer.

JOHNNY RUSSELL

Known as a total entertainer, Johnny was born in Roundaway, Mississippi, and grew up on healthy doses of cornbread, butter beans, fried okra, and the Grand Ole Opry. At age eighteen he recorded his song,

"In A Mansion Stands My Love," which led to Chet Atkins's signing him to RCA Records, where he released "Red Necks, White Socks, and Blue Ribbon Beer," "Catfish John," and "The Baptism of Jesse Taylor." But it was Buck Owens's recording of his "Act Naturally" that catapulted them both to fame. It went to #1 for Buck, and then the Beatles recorded it. The rest is history. Johnny died in 2001, during production of this book.

MIKE SNIDER

Born in Gleason, Tennessee, in 1961, Mike received his first banjo at the age of sixteen. By the age of twenty-two he took top honors at the National Banjo Championship. After debuting on the Grand Ole Opry, he appeared on TNN's *Nashville Now* and was a cast member on *Hee Haw* for seven seasons. After earning his Opry membership in 1990, he began starring in Opryland's *Mike Snider Show* a year later. One of contemporary country's most popular entertainers, Mike is recognized for his banjo skills, his distinctive Tennessee drawl, and his comic tales about his wife Sabrina, a.k.a., "Sweetie."

JIM STAFFORD

In 1974, Jim wrote and recorded his first chart song, "The Swamp Witch," following it with a gold single, "Spiders and Snakes" and several other hits, including "My Girl Bill," "Wildwood Weed," and "Cow Patti." His TV career was launched with *The Jim Stafford Show* on ABC in 1975. He co-hosted *Those Amazing Animals* with Burgess Meredith and Priscilla Presley; hosted fifty-six episodes of *Nashville on the Road*, and made twenty-six appearances on *The Tonight Show*. He wrote "Can't Get The Hell Out Of Texas" for George Jones and Jerry Reed. He now owns his own theater in Branson, Missouri, where he does 350 shows a year.

RAY STEVENS

When Ray Stevens says he just thinks funny, his key word is *thinks*. Like many revered American wits, from Charlie Chaplin to Bill Cosby, Stevens's humor is keenly observant and rich in nuance. Born Harold Ray

Ragsdale in Clarkdale, Georgia, in January, 1939, Ray came to Nashville in 1957 and recorded his first record at the old RCA "B" studio. In 1962, he came back to Nashville and worked on more than three hundred sessions as a pianist, arranger, and vocalist his first year. One of those sessions was his own "Ahab The Arab," which went to #5 pop. In 1970 he wrote "Everything Is Beautiful," which became his first #1 hit and won him a Grammy as Male Vocalist of the Year. In 1974 he hit #1 with "The Streak," and between 1975 and 1984 he won another Grammy for his arrangement of "Misty," had hits with "Shriner's Convention," "Mississippi Squirrel Revival," and "It's Me Again, Margaret." His video, *Comedy Video Classics*, released on his own Clyde Records, Inc., sold over two million copies.

GLENN SUTTON

A Louisiana native, Glenn moved to Nashville in 1964 and soon thereafter signed with Al Gallico Music. In the mid-'60s he and Billy Sherrill wrote hits for Wanda Jackson, Stonewall Jackson, Ferlin Husky, Tommy Cash, George Jones, and Tammy Wynette. In 1966, he and Sherrill earned BMI's Country Song of the Year for "Almost Persuaded," a #1 hit for David Houston. He wrote and performed "The Football Card" for Mercury Records. Along with twenty-seven BMI Awards and fourteen #1 singles, he has had recent cuts by Tracy Byrd and Gary Allan.

BONNIE TAGGERT

In the music business for twenty-five years, Bonnie was Director of Publicity and Artist Development at Warner Bros. Records and Capitol Records for seven years and five years, respectively. President of Creative Media for five years, she handled publicity for Chet Atkins and several other artists. For the past six years, she has been Marketing Director for the Vinny Pro-Celebrity Invitational/Electrolux USA Championship.

JOE TAGGERT

Called "ProJoe" for good reason, Joe is Chief Operating Officer of Tennessee PGA, Tennessee Golf Association, and the Tennessee Golf

Foundation. He oversees activities of all three associations, as well as the Vinny, which has been a high profile and successful fundraiser for junior golf. For two years he directed the Music City Pro-Celebrity Golf Tournament, and has won many awards, including Golf Professional of the Year, 1974 and 1977. Teamed with Vince Gill, he won the Tennessee PGA Pro-Am Championship in 1994. His best competitive round: 63!

MERLE TRAVIS

Chet Atkins said, "Merle could write you a hit song and sing it; he could draw you a cartoon; he could play you a great guitar solo; or he could fix your watch. There is a certain style to my playing which is the influence of the guitar picking of Merle Travis." Born in 1917 in Muhlenberg County, Kentucky, Merle performed all over the country in various bands while developing his unique guitar style. But it was his stint on radio station WLW in Cincinnati that brought him national fame. His songs added to his growing legend: "Divorce Me C.O.D." "Smoke, Smoke, Smoke That Cigarette," "Dark as a Dungeon," and the classic "Sixteen Tons." He died in 1983.

TOWNES VAN ZANDT

Townes Van Zandt wrote the classic, "Pancho and Lefty," recorded in 1983 by Willie Nelson and Merle Haggard, and is widely admired as one of the greatest country and folk artists of his generation.

JAY VERN

A Connecticut Yankee, Jay Vern landed in Nashville because of his love of music inherited from his grandfather, who came to this country from Sicily. Jay played keyboards with the Righteous Brothers' Bill Medley, with the Memphis Horns, and was Lorrie Morgan's arranger, bandleader, and keyboardist on the Opry when she was married to Keith Whitley. He now owns and operates a recording studio, Jay's Place, at 1508 17th Avenue South, in Nashville.

STEVE WARINER

Born in Indiana in 1954, by age seventeen Steve was bassist for Dottie West, at twenty-two for Bob Luman, and at twenty-four for Chet Atkins. He lists Chet as his greatest musical influence. After two decades as a professional musician, he was showered with honors for his #1 hit "Holes in the Floor of Heaven," co-written with Billy Kirsch. He has won two Grammy Awards, four CMA Awards, two ACM Awards, eleven BMI Songwriter Awards, thirty top ten songs, and more than a dozen #1s, including Garth Brooks's "Longneck Bottle." In 1999, he won Gibson Guitar's award as Best Male Country Guitarist.

HANK WILLIAMS

Hiram "Hank" Williams was born September 17, 1923, and had his first band, the Drifting Cowboys, at age thirteen. At age fourteen, he won an amateur night contest in Montgomery, Alabama, singing his "WPA Blues," which made him known around town as the "Hillbilly Shakespeare." In 1944, he married Audrey Mae Sheppard, who took him to Nashville to meet Fred Rose of Acuff-Rose Publishing. After releasing four songs, Hank became a star. When the Grand Ole Opry turned him down, he joined the *Louisiana Hayride* in 1948 and was an instant success. His recording of "Lovesick Blues" sold millions, so the Opry could no longer resist. He debuted on June 11, 1949, receiving a standing ovation and an unprecedented six encores. After Audrey divorced him and the Opry fired him in 1952, it's said Hank never drew another happy breath. But he managed to do magnificent recordings of three of his greatest songs, "Kawliga," "Your Cheatin' Heart," and "Take These Chains From My Heart." Thought by many to be country's greatest songwriter, he died on December 31, 1952, in the back seat of his '52 Cadillac.

SHEB WOOLEY

As an actor, Sheb has appeared in over seventy movies including *High Noon* with Gary Cooper and *Hoosiers* with Gene Hackman; too many TV shows to number, including *Rawhide, Hee Haw, The Dollmaker,* and

Murder, She Wrote; tons of singles and albums, including his own multi-million seller, "Purple People Eater," and Ray Stevens's hit, "The Day That Clancy Drowned"; and received CMA's Comedian of the Year Award as his alter ego, Ben Colder.

FARON YOUNG

Known as "The Sheriff," a name he got from one of eight movies he starred in, Faron was an original—great singer, businessman, entrepreneur. He could hold an audience in the palm of his hand, whether singing, telling a joke, or telling you off. His outspoken, outrageous nature was well known, which once caused Roger Miller to quip, "Faron's heart is as big as his mouth." He recorded over sixty albums, had eighty-nine charted singles, and forty-two top tens, including his #1 signature song, "Hello Walls." On December 10, 1996, Faron died of a self-inflicted gunshot wound. He was sixty-four years old.